The pastor of one of America's fastest growing churches tells you...

THERE'S A MIRACLE IN YOUR HOUSE

God's Solution Starts With What You Have

TOMMY BARNETT

CREATION
HOUSE

I would like to dedicate this book to:

*• my staff — people who were miracles
in my own congregation and have come to play
a very important role in church leadership;*

*• our deacons — they had more vision and daring
than I did and stretched me to believe God and
trust Him to provide for our financial needs;*

*• the people in my house, my congregation — they
helped carry out the dream God gave us;*

*• the miracle in my own house, my wife, Marja,
and our three children, Kristi, Matthew and Luke —
Matthew and Luke are both powerful
evangelists and preachers;
Kristi's goal has always been to have
a family and be a mother, and she's
given me three wonderful grandchildren;*

*• and my wonderful heavenly Father,
who is the source of all miracles.*

ACKNOWLEDGMENTS

❖

FOR THE writing of this book I am indebted in a tremendous way to the assistance of two men, Ron Hembree and Walter Walker.

Ron Hembree is an outstanding, award-winning author of many well-known books, including *St. Mark of Calcutta*; a TV personality; and a dear friend of many years who knows me as few people do. He took time out of his busy schedule to use his talents on this project, and I thank him.

Walter Walker, former editorial director of Creation House, heard me speak on this subject at the Charismatic Bible Ministries conference in 1991 in Tulsa and challenged me to write this book. Without his encouragement it never would have been written. He hounded me persistently until the dream became a reality. I appreciate his patience with my busy schedule and his helpful insights and teaching.

I would also like to thank the staffs of Creation House and my church for their hard work and patience in seeing this book become a reality.

CONTENTS

PREFACE

NOTHING BAD ever happens to you," the radio talk show host blurted out during an on-the-air interview with Tommy Barnett. She was so overwhelmed by the popular preacher's positive attitude she began to think he led some kind of charmed life immune from the petty problems plaguing the rest of us mere mortals.

Of course she was wrong, and Pastor Barnett quickly assured her he was very human and had faced his share of problems. "But," he said, "nothing bad ever does happen to me because our great God takes even the bad and makes it good. So, ultimately, you are right, even though there might be momentary misery and misunderstanding."

Ever since Tommy Barnett started storming through the country on his "special divine mission" over four decades ago, the world has had to sit up and take notice. His life and career have been such a series of miracles that many, like the radio host, wonder if he does lead a charmed existence. Like a perplexed physician seeks the cause of a mystery disease, many have probed and pondered the reasons for Tommy Barnett's success. Both critics and admirers have offered their opinions, but that is all they are — opinions.

Perhaps the best way to discover the answer to this enigma is to meet the man himself and get to know what lies beneath the polished exterior of this remarkable pastor. In doing so we discover the same flower of faith will bloom for all if we but learn and put into practice the great principles that were forged in the furnace of his life. This ordinary man has become quite extraordinary and insists that we can all grow far beyond ourselves if we really want to. He says, "The miracle is in the house!"

Those of us who have known Tommy Barnett through the years recognize his uniqueness and, at the same time, his "commonness." The thousands of pastors and leaders who attend his annual pastors' school leave far different from when they arrived. For us to touch this man's life is to touch the potential of greatness within ourselves.

This book seeks to capture the passions of this highly successful pastor-preacher. Tommy Barnett is consumed with advancing the kingdom of Jesus Christ through reaching the helpless, homeless and hurting of our world. He believes in "vicarious" success. That is, he believes all those God permits him to touch can do greater things than he has accomplished. It thrills him to see their success because his single passion is not recognition but that all men might come to know Jesus Christ.

Most want "magical" answers rather than spiritual ones. Not this unique man. Tommy Barnett rejects "pop psychology" and the various fads in the church. Rather he insists there are age-old, available and viable principles in God's Word giving us information and inspiration so we all can discover and unleash the miracle that is in the house. All those desiring to make the most of their potential would do well to hear and heed: The miracle you need right now is already within your grasp!

Ron Hembree
Phoenix, Arizona

8

ONE

Down and Out
in Davenport

THERE'S A miracle in the house!
I've said that to myself countless times in the face
of discouragement and opposition. As I persevered,
the miracle inevitably appeared.

In the midst of impossible situations I have just kept
saying, "There's got to be a miracle in the house!" And
God comes through — sometimes in ways I could never
have imagined.

I've preached it to others in our church here in Phoenix

and to the ministers in training in the Master's Commission. The staff and laypersons of our church have presented it to the six thousand Christian leaders who come to Phoenix each year to learn how we discovered that the miracle was in the house. And I've taught it to the more than a hundred businessmen I meet with every Thursday. As a result of this principle, lives, churches and businesses have exploded into a new dimension of fruitfulness and success. We've built a church with 180 successful outreach ministries to every group we can think of, from professional athletes to street people and bikers.

The same principles can work for you in your home, your job and your church or in any situation that calls for a miracle.

When we think of miracles, what comes to mind are the more spectacular brands of divine intervention such as the miracle of healing. Throughout this book I will use the term *miracle* in a broader sense to include God's protection, provision or direction.

When I say the miracle is "in the house," I don't necessarily mean in your phyical house. In chapter 2 you'll understand why I use that terminology.

To say the miracle is in the house means that the answer to your need begins with something that is already there in your grasp, in your ability or in your possession.

If God were always to fix our problems in the way we wanted Him to, the skies would be crowded with the provisions that were floating down right out of heaven. Most of the time God's miraculous provision for us in our need comes not so much like manna from heaven but in the multiplication of what we already have — fishes and loaves, for example.

When the challenges become overwhelming, God may say something to you like, How many fishes and loaves do you have?

Sometimes the key to miracles is in simply doing what

He says even though it goes against conventional wisdom — like casting the net on the other side of the boat.

When you doubt your own power and abilities to do what is required of you, He might ask you, as He did Moses, "What is that in your hand?"

The greatest miracle of your life might just begin with something that is already in the house or already in your hand.

You'll see what I mean by that a little later, but first of all I need to explain how the principle started to work in me. Like most great lessons, the learning experience began in the midst of a difficult situation.

WHEN I ARRIVED IN the small Iowa city my self-confidence was low. My dad had wanted me to stay with him in Kansas City as an associate pastor. But I had felt God stirring my heart to pastor my own church. I had been a "successful" evangelist since I was sixteen years old and had assumed that a church would want to grab me up right away. I thought I would be able to pick for myself which one of those large churches I would take.

It didn't hurt to have a successful pastor for a father, a man who had lots of friends and pull in the denomination. I had a lot going for me — so I supposed — as I confidently typed up my "impressive" resumé and sent out copies to all the large churches I heard were looking for a pastor.

But the demand for Tommy Barnett was all in my own imagination.

Not one church called. As the weeks passed I began to feel something must be really wrong. I swallowed my pride and applied for churches not quite as large as I thought I could handle. Surely they would want me, and I knew I could do them good. But they too ignored my gracious offer to become their pastor. Frankly, no one wanted me.

In a state of desperation one day I cried out, "God, no

matter what kind of door You open, I promise I will step through it." Within days I heard from Davenport, Iowa. The deacon who called to invite me to try out told me what a great church they had.

I felt I was meant for bigger places than Davenport, a sullen little settlement on the mighty Mississippi river. Nevertheless, I told God I would go through whatever door He opened. So off I went to the tryout in Davenport.

Arriving late Saturday evening, I drove all over town, wanting to take a first look at this great church. But it was nowhere to be found. Early the next morning I went looking again and eventually ended up on the wrong side of the tracks.

There it was — on Elsie Street, right behind A & W Root Beer. In my years as an evangelist I had seen every kind of church, but nothing like this. It was worse than the worst I had ever seen. I was suddenly reminded of my commitment to go through any door God would open.

It was an old, dilapidated building that had been around too long and constructed too cheaply even to pretend to be historic — and it smelled, too. It begged for a bulldozer to come and put it out of its misery.

The little wood-frame building seated fewer than a hundred and had high, concrete steps that were cracked in the middle. The faded paint was peeling, windows were broken, and the yard was unkempt. As I walked down the aisle, every board creaking under my feet, I noticed that the building was lit by bare light bulbs hanging from wires. The carpet had holes, and the building was heated by an old coal stove.

I remember when I was a kid playing marbles with my friends. If someone made a bad shot and yelled "overs" before he was called or caught, he got a second chance. I wanted to yell "overs" to God. Davenport was not my idea of an open door. But I had made a sacred vow so I had to say yes to the invitation at least to talk with the church board. In my heart I was sure God would not sentence me to such an unlikely place. After all, I had preached to thousands around the world.

If you pray for guidance and look for the open door but are not impressed with what you see (for example, taking a lesser job), *don't be too quick to write it off.* God's miracles are found behind some uninviting doors. We miss the miracles because we don't look in the places where God hides them.

> IT is the glory of God to conceal a matter,
> but the glory of kings is to search out a matter.
>
> Proverbs 25:2

Sunday morning dawned, and seventy-six people showed up for the service. This was considered an excellent number, apparently pumped up by the curiosity of those who wanted to take a gander at the prospective preacher.

That morning service didn't improve on my first impression. The song service was accompanied by an old, out-of-tune upright piano. The song leader didn't sing well either; on top of that, he led the little group in a chorus that sounded more like a dirge than praise. The people sang listlessly.

I was sure this Sunday in the Quad Cities was equivalent to Abraham's taking Isaac to Mount Moriah. It was only a test, and if I passed it I knew God would open some bright and beautiful door because I had been obedient.

I determined to preach the hardest sermon I knew just to discourage them from even considering me. I stared out at seventy-six of the most negative people I had ever seen and began to hack away at my message on faith. I must admit my heart was not into the subject. I just wanted to get through it and out of town so I could get on with whatever else lay ahead in my life.

The deacons wanted to meet with me that afternoon to interview me for the job. I obliged them because there was little else to do in Davenport but count the hours until I could escape back to the civilization of Kansas City.

That Sunday night I preached my "meanest" sermon and after the altar call set out for the door. I had already checked out of the motel so that I could leave for home immediately. The board stopped me short, saying I could not leave until the voting was over.

Voting?

Now it came to me. I was so preoccupied with my disappointment I had forgotten to tell them I was not going to take the church. They had already gathered the twenty members in the back room to decide my future.

I was stuck.

Pacing the floor, I tried my best to figure out a way to let them know they were wasting their time. I was never coming to Davenport, and that was that. But the board came out before I had time to put a workable plan together. They were all smiles, telling me I had received 100 percent of the votes, and this was the first time in the history of the church such a thing had happened. It must be God!

What they did not tell me was that no pastor had survived the church more than two years before he moved on or was moved by an unceremonious prodding from the same voting body that was so enthusiastically endorsing my candidacy.

It has always been hard for me to say no straight out, and the people were so excited I did not want to disappoint them. Therefore, I did the only thing I knew to do — I stalled. I told the church this was a great spiritual matter, and I had to pray it through before responding to their offer. It was indeed a grave spiritual matter, but in all honesty I was buying time so I could let them down easy. They swallowed their disappointment and assured me they understood. In spite of their assurances I knew they did not really understand, and they were wondering why I would not jump at the chance to be their pastor.

Returning to Kansas City I wrestled with God for three weeks telling Him all the reasons why Davenport was not a good idea for me. I had always envisioned myself preaching in New York or Los Angeles. I saw little opportunity in the town or in the church.

After three tormented weeks I called the board and told them I was on my way.

OUR FIRST DAYS IN Davenport were a struggle. No one came to the altar to accept Christ, and the evangelistic calling within me cried out that something was horribly wrong. I met with the deacons to tell them maybe it was not God's will for me to be there after all. I called my dad and complained. Both the board and my father said I should hold steady. This was especially hard for me after seeing hundreds respond to my altar calls when I was on the evangelistic field. But I stayed and prayed strictly out of sheer obedience rather than any great spiritual desire.

Up until this time everything had gone well with me and my ministry. Now I was stuck in a difficult situation. Perhaps if I could just endure it for a while, I would be out the door and on my way to bigger and better things. But God had another plan, and that was to give me victory in the face of immovable obstacles.

The answer did not come through my mighty sermons or any of the other things I tried in order to bring life into that church. In fact it was at the end of my efforts that I discovered that the miracle had been in the house all along.

I ate lunch with Mrs. Bobbie Stottlemeyer and her husband, Leon, my first Sunday in Davenport. She had been in the church for several months and had a real concern for the lost, but the seed inside her had never blossomed.

One day after I had exhausted all my ideas she came to me saying, "Brother Barnett, I've been saved for less than a year, and although I've never won anyone to the Lord,

I've been going out every Friday for two hours to witness. I believe God has led you to this city to help us win people to Christ."

There was something so sincere in her spirit that I asked if I could accompany her and her partner the next Friday when they went out to witness. She agreed, so I drove them on their rounds. The first week we had no success. But the second week that we went out witnessing I drove around the block after I had dropped the ladies off for their appointment. Not finding a parking place I pulled again in front of the targeted house, and one of the women beckoned to me frantically. I thought something must be desperately wrong because she was so excited and emotional.

"Hurry, Brother Barnett," she cried, as she gestured wildly. "We've got an old man on his knees, and he wants to get saved. What do we do next?" I went inside and helped the ladies lead this dear old man to the Lord.

The next Sunday the excited women brought their brand-new convert to church and put him on the front row. Our people were thrilled when he stood to testify.

Something strange and wonderful happened that very special Sunday so long ago. That little dry and dead Iowa church started to stir to new life. I took advantage of the moment and told the congregation we would go witnessing again the next week and anyone else who wanted to get in on this wonderful joy could join us. Four ladies did, and that week two elderly women came to know the Lord. The following Sunday they showed up in church, and we had them testify. The next Friday we had more people out soul-winning and more converts to share what had happened to them. Soon the converts filled the front rows of our church, and the whole congregation caught the soul-winning fever.

So many were being saved and now needed transportation that I began appealing to the congregation for help. The lady who had started it all filled her car each week with new converts and then commandeered her husband's vehicle. They both were making two trips to church every Sunday with our new babes in Christ.

I went to the church board to ask that we buy a bus, but the response was decidedly cool.

"We had a bus before you came," the members told me flatly. "It sat and rusted. No one would ride in it when it would run. We don't want a bus ministry."

"Men, this is not just transportation. This is winning souls," I appealed.

"Let's pray about it," they responded, throwing my own recent delaying ploy back in my face.

"We've prayed long enough," I blurted out. "Let's do something. If the Lord provides the money, will you let me buy a bus?"

They were trapped in the possibility they might just miss God if they gave a flat-out no. Not wanting to discourage their new pastor, the board conceded, "Well, if the Lord provides — but *only* if the Lord provides."

The next Sunday I asked all the people to stand if they had been saved in our witnessing program and had to depend on a ride to church. Then I added, "If anyone in the congregation feels inspired to buy a bus, please come to me after church."

Immediately Mrs. Stottlemeyer jumped up and said, "I don't have a thousand dollars to buy a bus, but I do have a house I have been trying to sell for months. If we sell this house, I will give you the money for the bus." We stopped the service right then and prayed.

A miracle occurred.

That week the woman sold her house, and the next Sunday she presented us with a check for our first bus.

We bought our bus, and now the battle was on. All hell wanted to stop this work before it started. Our bus motor burned up the very next week. I stood before the congregation to tell them the news and saw them shake their heads sagely, "We told you so." I did not dare ask for an

17

offering to repair the motor but went to the bank and borrowed the money myself to get the bus back on the road. Within a month the bus was jammed full, and we had to buy another.

One of our excited new members bought the second bus and then a third. "As long as God prospers me and as long as you keep filling them, I will buy you buses," he said. While he could not continue this generous offer for long, God used him to inspire faith that He would provide as long as we continued winning souls.

Soon all our buses were filled and revival was in full swing with people getting saved and packing out our little building. We had brightened up the place, and excitement was running high. Before long we were forced to new facilities, and the revival had captured the imagination of the whole city.

When revival broke out in Davenport, the news soon made it around the country. Sunday school records were shattered. People poured in from all over, and the media sat up and paid attention. Our church began to battle the porno shops and massage parlors and won, the first time such a victory had happened in the history of Davenport. Hundreds were saved in these special meetings, and lives were changed dramatically.

The remarkable Iowa revival never stopped, and each Sunday new and exciting things happened. Far from damaging my "reputation," Davenport made it. I now look back embarrassed that my faith in God's wise leading was so small. When I left Davenport, forty-seven buses were bringing people to church. Four thousand people were in Sunday school.

Looking back at those years, I am amazed that people perceived I had it all together. How wrong that perception was. When I went to Davenport, God had so humbled me that I did not think even those seventy-six people would stay with me very long. I was so insecure that if I saw someone absent, I would leave the platform during the song service, go to my office and call that person's home.

It was God's grace, not my dynamics, that made it all happen. At Davenport I learned a lesson that would form the fabric and foundation for the rest of my life and ministry. It was the simple awareness that the miracle is in the house!

EVERY STEP OF THE way and at every obstacle I found that the supply to meet my need began with something God had already put in the house. Pastors need to realize that everything they need to build a great church is already in their congregations. Mrs. Stottlemeyer was the miracle in the house at Davenport, and she has been followed by many more. Almost all of the full-time staff members who have worked with me over the years have come from within the church I was pastoring at the time.

Every businessman needs to recognize that the keys for his success are in his own hand or his own organization. In every child is the potential to become a miracle. In your house or in your life God has already planted the seeds that can blossom and become the answer to your most desperate dilemma.

Today I live in Phoenix, Arizona, a city in the middle of the desert. A seed can lie dormant in the dry sand for months and even years. But when the rain finally does come, the desert blooms like a garden.

That's the way it is with many people's lives. They feel they have been in a dry desert for so long that life appears to be gone. Yet life is everywhere, lying dormant, just waiting to come forth. Tiny seeds waiting to become something great — that's what Jesus said the kingdom of God was like.

AND He said, "How shall we picture the kingdom of God, or by what parable shall we present it?

19

³¹"It is like a mustard seed, which, when sown upon the soil, though it is smaller than all the seeds that are upon the soil,

³²"yet when it is sown, grows up and becomes larger than all the garden plants and forms large branches; so that the birds of the air can nest under its shade."

Mark 4:30-32

One pastor said to me, "You seem to have the ability to take nobodies and turn them into somebodies." The key is that I believe in people! I believe everyone has the seed in them to do something great for God. I believe it even when I can't see it. I know there's a miracle in there somewhere.

There was a man in the church in Davenport named Orbie Underwood. Orbie was a hard worker at a factory. He was a rather low-key kind of guy. But he was inspired by Mrs. Stottlemeyer. He took over a bus route, did a great job and saw his life begin to change.

Not only has Orbie been instrumental in bringing hundreds into the kingdom of God, but he has also become a deacon in the church. Orbie took the principles he learned in church and put them to practice in other areas of his life. Today Orbie Underwood has one of the most successful conversion van businesses in the quad cities and state.

In the years that followed those early days in Davenport I learned a lesson over and over: Whenever I come to difficult situations in the church or in my personal life, I just need to look for the seed of the miracle that is already in the house. I hope you too can discover that the miracle you need is already in your grasp.

Through the experience in Davenport I discovered the ten commandments for the making of a miracle. That's chapter 2.

Tell Me —
What Do You Have
in the House?

OUT OF my deep need I learned to lean on God and started to see His sufficiency in each situation. Davenport was a wonderful education. My insecurity was not pleasant at the time, but God used it to teach me things about faith I could not have learned at any other place or time.

In that little Iowa town one vivid Bible story was brought to mind over and over. God was showing me what was to become the key to the series of miracles that would guide my life and give me success beyond anything I had imagined. It was the familiar and simple story of the worried widow with the unpaid bill.

NOW a certain woman of the wives of the sons of the prophets cried out to Elisha, "Your servant my husband is dead, and you know that your servant feared the Lord; and the creditor has come to take my two children to be his slaves."

²And Elisha said to her, "What shall I do for you? *Tell me, what do you have in the house?*" And she said, *"Your maidservant has nothing in the house except a jar of oil."*

³Then he said, "Go, borrow vessels at large for yourself from all your neighbors, even empty vessels; do not get a few.

⁴"And you shall go in and shut the door behind you and your sons, and pour out into all these vessels; and you shall set aside what is full."

⁵So she went from him and shut the door behind her and her sons; they were bringing the vessels to her and she poured.

⁶And it came about when the vessels were full, that she said to her son, "Bring me another vessel." And he said to her, "There is not one vessel more." And the oil stopped.

⁷Then she came and told the man of God. And he said, "Go, sell the oil and pay your debt, and you and your sons can live on the rest."

2 Kings 4:1-7, italics added

At least ten great principles in this simple story have revolutionized my life. For me, this story speaks of the ten commandments for the making of a miracle. Here they are:

1. Know Where to Go When You Don't Know What to Do.

She was a widow and a single parent in an impossible situation with no food and no means of support. She was being threatened by angry bill collectors. If she did not pay up immediately, she would lose her children.

The only thing going for her was that she knew where to turn. Only God could make a miracle happen in her situation. She went to the prophet with her plight.

Where we place our expectations determines whether we receive a miracle. If we insist on looking to man to supply our needs, we will continue to be disappointed. The major battles of life are spiritual so there must be spiritual resources if things are to turn around.

We would do well to remember King Asa's downfall. When threatened by hostile forces, this ancient king put his trust in Syria rather than God. His plan of action was to pay King Ben-hadad to send his troops as mercenaries to protect him. The prophet reprimanded him saying,

THE eyes of the Lord search back and forth across the whole earth, looking for people whose hearts are perfect toward him, so that he can show his great power in helping them.

2 Chronicles 16:9, TLB

God wants to show Himself strong on your behalf as well. But going to God means asking, praying and believing you have received. Paul exhorted the Philippians to worry about nothing and to pray about everything (Phil. 4:6). Our worrying is most often expressed by an ongoing, inner conversation we have with ourselves. We will argue, complain and moan about the situation just as if someone were actually listening. That's why when someone asks us sincerely how we are doing, that person gets such an earful. The complaint has been well rehearsed.

23

THE TEN COMMANDMENTS FOR THE MAKING OF A MIRACLE

I.
Know Where to Go When You
Don't Know What to Do.

II.
Don't Seek an Earthly Messiah.

III.
Find Out What's in the House.

IV.
Don't Be Blinded by Negativism,
but Pass on to the Positive.

V.
Faith Is Not Faith Until You Do
Something — Action Is Required.

VI.
Don't Put Limitations on
God's Ability to Provide.

VII.
Shut the Door on Doubt.

VIII.
Pour Until There Is No More.

IX.
Move Beyond the Miracle.

X.
Remember: There Will Always Be Enough.

Looking to God in the midst of your troubles means that you stop rehearsing your complaints and turn that inner conversation into upward prayer. That's when faith begins.

2. Don't Seek an Earthly Messiah.

Elisha gives the widow a surprising answer when she tells him her plight. "What shall I do?" Elisha asked. His reaction to the widow at first seems to suggest frustration that she had come to him. He seemed to be saying, What do you want me to do about it? I believe he was simply refusing to let her put her trust in him, insisting she keep it in the Lord.

Unfortunately, Christianity is very celebrity oriented.

"If I could just talk to Pastor Jones."

"If I could just get Prophet Smith to pray for me, I know God would meet my need."

As Christians we should seek to touch the hem of Jesus' garment — no one else's.

Elisha knew he could not help the widow with his own limited resources. But he did help her keep her faith properly focused.

A man in the church came to me one day in a difficult situation. Before he was saved he had committed a felony and was about to go on trial. He could plead innocent, as his lawyer recommended, and easily get off. Or he could face the consequences of admitting his guilt. He desperately wanted me to make the decision for him. Of course, I could only point him to Jesus.

He got the direction from the Lord firsthand and was shown what to do. He pleaded guilty. But God turned events around so that, instead of spending the next five years in prison, he became one of the most successful businessmen in the church. God's grace and plan were worked out because he heard for himself and obeyed.

Elisha was pointing the needy widow to the source of

her miracle. God's wisdom and God's help far surpass anything anyone else can do for you. So always seek Him and put your trust in Him.

3. Find Out What's in the House.

Like the needy widow we get so caught up in what we don't have that we do not see the possibilities in what we already have. Elisha, after redirecting the widow's faith, asks, "What do you have in the house?" She did not need a new vision of her need. She was well aware of that. What she needed was to recognize that God had already given her the beginnings for her miracle, even though what she had seemed so small.

When I went to Davenport I had no idea the seeds of a miracle resided in that little, lackluster church. But God had put Mrs. Stottlemeyer there as a seed lying dormant. Finally, He opened my eyes to see that mighty miracles were in that unlikely little house.

4. Don't Be Blinded by Negativism, but Pass on to the Positive.

Our first reaction to crisis is always negative. Nothing is good or right, and there's no hope. That was the widow's frame of mind when she replied, "Your maidservant has nothing in the house except a jar of oil."

The widow started out in the negative but quickly passed to the positive. Nothing could be more important! When you look to the God of possibilities you suddenly pass from the natural to the supernatural. It would have been very easy and very natural for the woman to have simply said, "Your maidservant has nothing in the house — period, paragraph and end of story. Now what are you, Mr. Prophet, going to do about it?"

It's easy to say, "I have nothing." But it takes faith to go on and say, "Nothing but a jar of oil, one small possibility, one small asset, one insignificant thing I can offer for God to use and multiply."

Faith does not deny present reality. It just acknowledges that all things are possible with God. It serves no purpose to say a problem does not exist or that the miracle has happened when it has not. You only deceive yourself.

Faith in God does, however, change how you see things.

"Nothing *but* a jar of oil."

"*Nevertheless*, at Your word we will let down the net."

These statements were made by people who looked the problems square in the face. But it was their faith that enabled them to see beyond the difficulties to the possibilities. Doubt will cause you to say: "We have nothing."

Or maybe: "We've already tried that, and it didn't work."

Miracles begin with faith, and it takes faith to break through the negativism and see the seed you have to cultivate. If you don't look with eyes of faith, small blessings are too little to recognize. So you say, "There's nothing in the house."

During those first few weeks in Davenport when I went to the board and to my dad, suggesting to them that I had missed the will of God, they wisely held my feet to the fire until I passed from the negative to the positive. I shudder to think what would have happened to me and the direction of my life if I had stayed in my negativism refusing to see the possibilities in that little river town. Thank God for the "Elishas" in my life who helped me move from the natural to the supernatural.

The fact is that we always have far more available to us than we think. Pass on to the positive.

5. Faith Is Not Faith Until You Do Something — Action Is Required.

Diagnosis is no cure although it is the first step toward health. There must be follow-up treatment if wellness is to come. Thus, Elisha told the widow she had to take some action to get out of her fix. She was to go out and borrow as many vessels as she could find. Remember two-thirds of the word *God* is *go*. And there is always a *go* in the gospel! She had to get active if she was to experience a miracle.

Most people want God to act on their behalf, but first they must act by faith on their own behalf. Israel wandered forty years in the wilderness because the people failed to take action when God instructed them to move forward.

Unbelief is not expressed so much by what people do as by what they do not do. Every supernatural victory won by Israel when they finally did enter the promised land under Joshua was accompanied by some corresponding action on their part — some faith offering of their own resources that God anointed and blessed.

6. Don't Put Limitations on God's Ability to Provide.

"What's that silly widow woman going to do with all of those pots?" her neighbors must have said. "She's finally lost her mind."

Of course, when you are as desperate for a miracle as this woman was, you'll do just about anything. The man of God said to her:

> GO, borrow vessels at large for yourself from all your neighbors, even empty vessels; do not get a few.
>
> 2 Kings 4:3

Get as many as you can, and get them from everywhere, the prophet was saying. I wonder if the woman had any idea of what was about to happen. In any case she obeyed the prophet.

In the spiritual world we must attempt things so big for

God that unless He helps us we will fall flat on our faces. Only then will He get full credit for what is accomplished, and only then will this knowledge keep us humbly aware that but for His blessings we are nothing (John 15:5). It is His work and His success — not ours.

God works through our positive expectations. It seems as if Elisha was dealing regularly with people about this.

WHEN Elisha became sick with the illness of which he was to die, Joash the king of Israel came down to him and wept over him and said, "My father, my father, the chariots of Israel and its horsemen!"

15And Elisha said to him, "Take a bow and arrows." So he took a bow and arrows.

16Then he said to the king of Israel, "Put your hand on the bow." And he put his hand on it, then Elisha laid his hands on the king's hands.

17And he said, "Open the window toward the east," and he opened it. Then Elisha said, "Shoot!" And he shot. And he said, "The Lord's arrow of victory, even the arrow of victory over Aram; for you shall defeat the Arameans at Aphek until you have destroyed them."

18Then he said, "Take the arrows," and he took them. And he said to the king of Israel, "Strike the ground," and he struck it three times and stopped.

19So the man of God was angry with him and said, "You should have struck five or six times, then you would have struck Aram until you would have destroyed it. But now you shall strike Aram only three times."

2 Kings 13:14-19

Elisha was angry with Joash because his response lacked faith and passion. You can't do great things if you don't attempt great things. Shooting the arrows was for

Joash what collecting the pots was for the widow. Again, God works with us according to our expectations or the lack of them.

When I was in Phoenix years later, the board of elders wanted the new church to seat ten thousand. I felt more comfortable with three thousand. They had much more faith than I. One day one of the deacons and I were watching Pat Robertson's "700 Club."

"You pastors are building your churches too small!" exclaimed Pat. "In fact, there's one pastor listening right now who is planning far too small." The deacon's elbow was planted firmly in my side.

We settled on a sixty-five-hundred-seat auditorium. It was filled as soon as we finished it. The deacons were right. Ten thousand was the right size. God filled the vessel that we brought Him.

7. Shut the Door on Doubt.

A key factor in this miracle story is what happened after the widow had borrowed the empty pots from her curious neighbors. Elisha told her, "And you shall go in and shut the door behind you and your sons." There will always be plenty of naysayers — those who say, "Precedent is against it." "We've tried before and failed." Or, "We can't afford it." Elisha simply insisted she shut out the skeptics and be deaf to doubt.

The widow's neighbors, who were fully aware of her plight, would think her actions were eccentric and would ridicule what she was doing. They would insist she was foolish to believe in something so impractical as what the prophet proposed. The fact is that many miracles are stillborn because doubt was invited into the delivery room.

Jesus cautioned, "Consider carefully what you hear" (Mark 4:24, NIV). He knew we act on and react to what we hear from those around us. Elisha also knew how quickly seeds of doubt grow in the soil of human depravity and despair. Therefore, he told the widow to go into her house and close the door to doubt. Like Mary, the mother of our Lord, we must ponder some dreams in our hearts rather than see them killed cruelly in casual conversation. Jesus said clearly,

DO not give dogs what is sacred; do not throw your pearls to pigs. If you do, they may trample them under their feet, and then turn and tear you to pieces.

Matthew 7:6, NIV

8. Pour Until There Is No More.

The widow provided the effort while God made the miracle. As she poured, the oil flowed. We can only surmise she had borrowed every available empty vessel in her little town. If there had been more vessels, there would have been more oil.

In Davenport where we began and now in Phoenix we are continuing to pour because the needs of the whole town have not been met. When all the vessels were full, the miracle ceased. Much of my time is spent looking for empty vessels to fill — hurting people to pour into. And the exciting thing is that provision continues to come as we continue to pour.

This does not mean we do not have money problems. There will always be the constant struggle against the god of this world. But, miraculously, the provision comes as we continue to step out in faith to reach out in love. I believe the oil of anointing will only stop when every empty vessel in our world is filled or when we stop offering up empty vessels. And I do not see that happening soon. We will pour until there is no more! The promise is:

NOW He who supplies seed to the sower and bread for food, will supply and multiply your seed for sowing and increase the harvest of your righteousness.

2 Corinthians 9:10

9. Move Beyond the Miracle.

Sadly, some are so mystified by the miracle that they get locked in place and fail to move on. A significant part of this story notes,

THEN she came and told the man of God. And he said, "Go, sell the oil and pay your debt, and you and your sons can live on the rest."

2 Kings 4:7

It was not enough for her to witness the miracle. There had to be purpose in it.

God gives great miracles for divine purpose — not just for our entertainment. Clearly the widow was not to get so wrapped up in the wonder that she forgot the purpose.

Miracles are so mighty that we often are tempted to glorify them rather than get on with the work of the kingdom. Miracles are meant not to dazzle us but to facilitate the Great Commission of Jesus Christ.

10. Remember: There Will Always Be Enough.

One of the most comforting principles of this great story came when Elisha told the widow, "You and your sons can live on the rest." God had given enough to assure that their family needs would always be met.

After I left Davenport I was to move on to another challenge. At first I thought what had happened in Iowa was a one-time occurrence. I didn't expect that it would ever happen again. But what was to happen next made Davenport look small.

32

❖

Being Led to
Your Next Miracle

ONE DAY I finally admitted that I had lost the conscious presence of God.

In spite of all the wonderful things I had been learning and the remarkable success of Davenport, the last few months had been deeply disturbing. There was a dryness in my relationship with God, and I couldn't figure out why. There was no great sin in my life or tension in the family or church. Things were going very well, and everyone around me was excited. My needs were all being met, and the church was easy to pastor. I had grown to love these people dearly. But I felt my preaching was mechanical and the spark gone.

I had lost the sense of God's presence. Oh, He was there, but it seemed as if I was just tuned out. I prayed, fasted and stayed up all night seeking God, but nothing changed.

There I was again, down and out in Davenport.

It was not because of failure but, ironically, because of success. And I did not know what to do to dig out.

I was in this dark mood when the letter came.

The letter was an invitation to be interviewed by the board of First Assembly of God in Phoenix, Arizona. At that point in my life I felt the last thing I needed was another church and another challenge. So I threw the letter in the wastebasket.

Again I was wrong.

Not only did Phoenix need me, but I needed them!

After several torturous days, I returned to the wastebasket. Fortunately, the janitor had not emptied my trash. I dug deep into the office garbage to retrieve the wadded-up paper. Ironing the crumpled letter out on my desk, I leaned over and prayed desperately with my head buried in my hands. Maybe, just maybe, God was speaking to me through my restlessness, and I was not listening.

Could it be that I would sense the nearness of God's presence again only if I followed whatever little lead there seemed to be? Somewhere I had read that while a flashlight shines only a short distance in front, the light extends further as you continue to walk. Maybe this would happen to me if I followed the little light I saw. That little light seemed to be this letter.

Ready to Move When the Brook Dries Up

NOW Elijah the Tishbite, who was of the settlers of Gilead, said to Ahab, "As the Lord, the

God of Israel lives, before whom I stand, surely there shall be neither dew nor rain these years, except by my word."

²And the word of the Lord came to him, saying,

³"Go away from here and turn eastward, and hide yourself by the brook Cherith, which is east of the Jordan.

⁴"And it shall be that you shall drink of the brook, and I have commanded the ravens to provide for you there."

⁵So he went and did according to the word of the Lord, for he went and lived by the brook Cherith, which is east of the Jordan.

⁶And the ravens brought him bread and meat in the morning and bread and meat in the evening, and he would drink from the brook.

⁷And it happened after a while, that the brook dried up, because there was no rain in the land.

⁸Then the word of the Lord came to him, saying,

⁹"Arise, go to Zarephath...."

1 Kings 17:1-9

I DIALED THE CHURCH board and made arrangements to fly to Phoenix for the meeting.

When I met with the Phoenix board I immediately knew the reason for my restlessness. Here was where God wanted me, and if I had not experienced such inner agitation I would not have even considered the move. I had everything I wanted in Davenport, and I loved the people dearly. When other churches called asking me to consider their pulpits, I turned them down without even giving them a second thought. God knew that I was a lot like Elijah. I would not listen to His leading unless my river dried up, forcing me to seek hard for His face and will.

The story of Elijah at the brook Cherith is full of surprises. I have come to understand that God's process of miracle making is accompanied by a never-ending series of unusual and unexpected things. Elijah is a good example of how God leads us into the making of a miracle.

A Surprising Place

Elijah delivered devastating news — that the nation of Israel would be crippled by a drought and famine. God knew that wicked King Ahab would be more inclined to kill the messenger than heed the message. The Bible reports,

> AND the word of the Lord came to him [Elijah], saying,
> ³"Go away from here and turn eastward, and hide yourself by the brook Cherith, which is east of the Jordan."
>
> 1 Kings 17:2-3

This was a surprising place since Elijah had just announced a famine. In a famine a brook dries up first, and yet it was there God sent Elijah, rather than to a full river where he could survive safely in drought.

In my own life I have always been surprised at where God sends me. I was reluctant when I went to Davenport, and although Phoenix was God's choice for my life, it would not have been my first choice. Even in my daily appointments I discover God often diverts me to surprising places in surprising ways where great things are done for Him.

A casual conversation or a "coincidental" meeting can be life changing. It is exciting and challenging to see what surprising places God will send me in the days ahead. I am learning to follow the Good Shepherd rather than take the lead. I only wish I were a better learner.

After spending a few years in Phoenix I found myself being diverted to another surprising place. I found myself at city hall. It seems the whole town had gathered together at city hall — local television news media, reporters, the city council, representatives from several commissions, the mayor and hundreds of others assembled. What most of them wanted was to tar and feather Tommy Barnett and run him out of town on a rail. I'll tell you more about that in a later chapter. But what seemed to be a place and a situation I would have avoided at all cost, turned into a surprising miracle.

A Surprising Provider

The second surprise in this story is whom, or what, God told to cater the prophet's food.

YOU shall drink of the brook, and I have commanded the ravens to provide for you there.
1 Kings 17:4

If we are going to receive "heavenly" food, surely we would expect an angelic catering service. Yet God told Elijah he would be fed by dirty birds.

Eight or more species of ravens are found in Israel. All are considered unclean by Hebrew law and feed on carcasses. Noah used a raven as the first bird to send out after the flood (Gen. 8:7). It did not return, perhaps finding floating carcasses on which to light and feed. The raven and the vulture are grouped in the same disgusting class in Proverbs (Prov. 30:17, NIV). It was probably a shock to Elijah to learn his "angel's food" would be delivered in such suspicious fashion. In fact, it took real faith to eat whatever was brought to him, and only a real saint could see ravens' food as provision from God.

The symbolism in this story is striking. It simply shows how God can and will provide from unusual sources by surprising means. The kingdoms of this world can and will become the kingdoms of our God. Therefore, I fully expect many of the provisions for the church and God's people in these days to come from the world.

One year as we were preparing for our Feed-the-Multitude Thanksgiving celebration, the regional manager of a national fast-food, fried chicken company was touched by what we were doing. He then provided three thousand drumsticks for the meals for our bus children that day, and has done so every year since. Incidentally, as he provided, the Lord provided for him, and he married a woman in our church less than a year later.

When the Israelites lived in the land of Canaan, they were threatened constantly. Sometimes the situation looked hopeless. Finally, they turned to God for help. Revival came to Judah after Jehoshaphat turned the nation to God's Word. The writer of Chronicles notes how it affected the surrounding nations.

NOW the dread of the Lord was on all the kingdoms of the lands which were around Judah, so that they did not make war against Jehoshaphat.

[11]And some of the Philistines brought gifts and silver as tribute to Jehoshaphat; the Arabians also brought him flocks, 7,700 rams and 7,700 male goats.

2 Chronicles 17:10-11

A Surprising Problem

Elijah experienced success and rest at the little brook. His needs were met, and things were going very well. The great prophet was safe and secure by the brook just as I was in Davenport. He probably had adjusted to his unusual servers and may have even developed a friendly relationship with the accommodating birds. Elijah had no move on his agenda. Then a surprising problem arose — the brook dried up! My brook in Davenport dried up too.

It was not some mid-life crisis but simply God nudging me to move on.

One of the hardest lessons in life is to learn that God calls us to a place for a reason and for a season. We want to settle at some comfortable place forever because it is "safe." But life is like a twisting river. Sometimes we stop on a beautiful bank and loll there for some time. But if we do not get back in the stream, we miss the exciting things around the next bend.

If Elijah's supply had not dried up, he might have missed the mighty miracles that lay ahead. He would not have had the dramatic encounter on Mount Carmel in which the fire of God descended (1 Kin. 18:38). He would have missed the supernatural end of the famine, the angel's touch, and his final fantastic ride to heaven in the whirlwind (1 Kin. 18:45, 19:5; 2 Kin. 2:11).

Most of all, he would have missed his role in God's plan to save a precious widow and her son from starvation. Elijah's surprising problem was only a prod to move him on to another area of ministry.

We live in a transient society, largely as a result of the job market. Often when Christians go into a new job, a door has opened miraculously. And when they leave a job, it is almost always because of an accumulation of problems. Going in is filled with excitement and new possibilities. Going out is usually accompanied with stress and tension, that is, until the next door opens.

That's how it is in life and in business. That's also how it was with Elijah. If it hadn't been for the accumulation of things leading up to his departure, he may have missed God's leading to his next miracle.

A Surprising Directive

THEN the word of the Lord came to him, saying,
⁹"Arise, go to Zarephath, which belongs to Sidon, and stay there; behold, I have commanded a

39

widow there to provide for you."

¹⁰So he arose and went to Zarephath, and when he came to the gate of the city, behold, a widow was there gathering sticks; and he called to her and said, "Please get me a little water in a jar, that I may drink."

¹¹And as she was going to get it, he called to her and said, "Please bring me a piece of bread in your hand."

¹²But she said, "As the Lord your God lives, I have no bread, only a handful of flour in the bowl and a little oil in the jar; and behold, I am gathering a few sticks that I may go in and prepare for me and my son, that we may eat it and die."

1 Kings 17:8-12

AGAIN, THE INSTRUCTIONS OF God are surprising from a human standpoint. Why did He call on a widow to feed Elijah? Widows had no means of support, especially this widow.

The story of Elijah and the Sidonian widow of Zarephath is similar to the encounter that Elijah's successor, Elisha, had with a widow. Both widows were despairing for their lives and the lives of their children. They both also found out that the miracle they needed was already in the house. They only had to recognize it and activate it.

At the beginning of His public ministry in Galilee, Jesus highlighted how improbable it was for God to send Elijah to this widow. After having read from the scroll on the Sabbath, Jesus was teaching those who had come that day to the synagogue. Luke's Gospel says that they were all speaking well of Him and wondering at His gracious words — that is, until He mentioned Elijah and the widow of Zarephath.

AND He said, "Truly I say to you, no prophet is welcome in his home town.

[25]"But I say to you in truth, there were many widows in Israel in the days of Elijah, when the sky was shut up for three years and six months, when a great famine came over all the land;

[26]"and yet Elijah was sent to none of them, but only to Zarephath, in the land of Sidon, to a woman who was a widow."

Luke 4:24-26

How did those in the synagogue react to this? Luke goes on to say that they were all filled with rage when they heard these words and immediately tried to kill Jesus by casting Him off a cliff!

Being sent to the widow of Zarephath was more than an unconventional surprise. It was unthinkable.

GOD'S PLAN FOR ELIJAH was a surprise not only because the Sidonians were considered pagans and idol worshippers. Why would a man of Elijah's stature and anointing have to be supplied by one in such need herself? God asked the prophet to go to a place of want and put a heavier burden on that household. It just didn't make sense.

Whatever you need, give that away to someone else. Every Sunday I stand at the front door to shake hands and hug everybody who will let me.

One person said to me, "Pastor Barnett, you sure are a loving person."

"No," I replied, "it's just that I need to be loved so much myself. So I'm just giving away what I need!" The opportunity to give turned out to be a blessing for the widow. It was also the beginning of her miracle.

God had already told the widow that the man of God was coming, and she would be the supply for his need (1 Kin. 17:9). By acting in accordance with God's surprise directive, she reaped what she sowed many times over.

A Surprising Request

THEN Elijah said to her, "Do not fear; go, do as you have said, but make me a little bread cake from it first, and bring it out to me, and afterward you may make one for yourself and for your son.

[14]"For thus says the Lord God of Israel, 'The bowl of flour shall not be exhausted, nor shall the jar of oil be empty, until the day that the Lord sends rain on the face of the earth.' "

1 Kings 17:13-14

THE PROPHET MADE A startling request. One might expect sympathy from this man of God, but all the woman received was what seemed to be a selfish demand: "Use your last oil and flour to feed me first."

What do you suppose went through the widow's mind? Maybe she thought sarcastically, Great, give the preacher our last meal — then we can eat.

Maybe she said to herself, Well, we're going to die anyway. What difference is one last meal? We might as well give it to the prophet and see what happens.

There's no way of knowing what the widow was thinking. We do know that the Scriptures say that God had commanded her to provide for the prophet. What she had was a command from God and a promise from the prophet.

As the old hymn says, "Trust and obey, for there's no other way...."[1]

A Surprising Miracle

SO she went and did according to the word of Elijah, and she and he and her household ate for many days.

[16]The bowl of flour was not exhausted nor did

the jar of oil become empty, according to the word
of the Lord which He spoke through Elijah.

1 Kings 17:15-16

The answer to a desperate need came from a "miracle
in the house." Miracles are not magic — but multiplication. Obedience to His Word and faith in His promise put
what we have into the Lord's hands so it can be multiplied. Then the miracle occurs. Just as a farmer must not
eat the seed, so we must sow the seed and look for Him to
multiply it.

Bringing what we have to the Lord to use and multiply
is as true for us today as it was for the two widows. This
is a law of the kingdom. Jesus said:

GIVE, and it will be given to you; good measure,
pressed down, shaken together, running over,
they will pour into your lap. For by your standard of measure it will be measured to you in return.

Luke 6:38

What do we give? That which we have. Where do we
find it? Somewhere in our house.

FOUR

What's That
in Your Hand?

MOSES CRINGED every time a whip cracked against a trembling Hebrew slave's back. Growing up in the house of Pharaoh's daughter, he never knew the cruelty of the slave drivers, but he was tormented inside. Why did his people have to suffer so much?

A botched attempt at revenge on a slave driver sent him running for his life, and he ended up tending livestock on the back side of the desert. One question haunted him continually: "God, why don't You help them?"

Finally God said to Moses, via the burning bush, "Why don't *you* deliver them, Moses?" But Moses wasn't eager to be a part of that plan.

> WHO am I that I should go to Pharaoh, and that I should bring the sons of Israel out of Egypt?"...
>
> [1]"What if they will not believe me, or listen to what I say? For they may say, 'The Lord has not appeared to you.' "
>
> [2]And the Lord said to him, "*What is that in your hand?*"
>
> Exodus 3:11, 4:1-2, italics added

Some people, like Moses, see a need and ask, "What do I have to offer in the face of such a challenge?" These people do nothing. But God said to Moses: "Look at what you have in your hand right now. You can take what you have and use it to meet the need — if you let Me help you."

The key to greatness is seeing the need and letting God use what is in your hand. There has been no better example of this to me than my own mother.

THE BARNETTS CAME FROM a strong and sturdy stock of old-fashioned Pentecostals and hard-shelled Baptists. Dad's mother was proud that she was a first cousin to President Woodrow Wilson's second wife, Edith Boling Galt. Mrs. Galt had been the widow of a Washington, D.C., jeweler when she and the president married following the death of his first wife. Later, when Wilson was struck down by a debilitating stroke, Edith "ran the government," guiding the ailing president's hand as he signed official documents.

Dad had inherited all the grit and gumption from the

Barnetts and used these well during his long and prosperous ministry. My mother's fine family hailed from England. Her grandfather had been the pastor of a large and historic Presbyterian church. Mom's life was all joy, just like her name, until her adored father died of double pneumonia when she was just eleven years old. From that day until she met and married my dad, she felt cheated because such a huge part of her life was grabbed away. To make matters worse, Mom was shunted off to a Bible school by her new stepfather who wanted her out of the way. While the pain of this rejection was intense and the sorrow deep, it was at that school she met my dad.

Enid, Oklahoma, sits glumly in the middle of the great Red Beds Plains that extend from Kansas to Texas. Here the soft red sandstone and shale lie shallow under the grassy soil. And it was here, at Southwestern Bible School, that love and destiny awaited young Hershel Barnett and lovely Joy Patten.

On the special day that Mom and Dad met, the boys of the Bible school were playing baseball while the girls strolled over the tiny campus of the struggling institution. The rules of this "holiness" Bible school were so strict that the faculty forbade any contact between the sexes. Boys and girls were even instructed to walk in opposite directions and could only speak while passing. They were severely reprimanded if they stopped to talk, much less date or hold hands.

Then it happened.

Suddenly a baseball smashed across the playing field onto the sidewalk and slammed into a pretty young girl. The ball struck so sharply that she doubled over with pain and crumpled onto the sidewalk. The ball hit the precise location where a still tender incision from an appendectomy was healing slowly. Girlfriends hovered over the fallen girl, and a young, handsome ball player dashed off the field to help.

Their eyes met.

46

Love was born in that moment.

Both Hershel and Joy knew — and both would express later — that something fateful and wonderful had happened in that first brief encounter. The boy walked away in a daze after making sure she was OK. He told his buddies, "That's the girl I'm going to marry." Later on he learned she left saying to her girlfriends, "That's the man I'm going to marry." The pain from the baseball soon faded, but the memory of that special encounter lingered.

Romance had little chance to blossom under the sharp eyes of the fussy faculty. Students were told young preachers must prioritize their Bs. First, they must get their books, then a Buick and finally a bride. If they ever got these out of order, there would be trouble, so said the older and "wiser" heads.

That first year after their brief encounter Hershel and Joy had little chance to speak to each other, but both harbored a secret inside: "This is the person I will marry." That awesome, unspoken awareness never left, even though there were the usual teenage fleeting flirtations and fantasies with others. And, in spite of the strict Bible school rules, young men and women will still be young men and women. There are always creative ways to communicate and circumvent unreasonable laws when a couple is in love. These Bible school kids had discovered such a way.

One day as the girls marched into the dining room, Joy felt a hand reach over her shoulder to take her fancy handkerchief. The drab school uniforms permitted only one accessory, and that was a fancy handkerchief fluffed out of the blouse pocket. Hershel grinned sheepishly and neatly tucked the feminine handkerchief into his own jacket pocket, arranging the tatted edges so they would show. This "mating rite" was commonly recognized among the students at the strict school. It meant Joy was now his girl if she did not grab the handkerchief back.

She did not.

The one time that afforded an approved way to talk to the opposite sex was at meals. The boys and girls had the luxury of sitting at the same tables, though the assigned seating arrangements were changed monthly. This gave the two young lovers opportunities to get to know each other and spend time conversing. They would make the most of each meal together, lingering so long that they drew disapproving glances from the faculty.

By the time graduation came, Hershel and Joy had grown strong in their commitment to each other even though they had not had the opportunity to date. As school closed, Joy wrote her first poem:

> After I think and think of you,
> Wondering just how or what to do,
> To make our love a lasting song,
> One that will last for years to come,
> Something whispers softly to me,
> "God is the Author of things to be."

Summer came, and school was finally out. Joy reluctantly returned home to Ponca City, Oklahoma, while Texan Barnett went back to Electra. The two kept in touch by letter, with Joy writing at the bottom, "Delight thyself also in the Lord; and he shall give thee the desires of thine heart" (Ps. 37:4, KJV). She admits, "I was hoping, of course, I was that desire."

She was.

On March 21, 1935, Hershel Barnett and Joy Patten were married.

Through the years Dad and Mom made a powerful team. There were many successes and some failures, but this dynamic duo always plunged ahead — innovating, invigorating and inciting passion for God wherever they went. It was in a little town in Texas that my mother discovered the positive power of pain.

The young evangelist and his new wife were seeing

phenomenal results. Crowds jammed the little church. Many souls were being saved and blessed. On the last night of this great meeting, the district superintendent of the Assemblies of God and the presbyter of the local section came calling. These were the men who had the power and influence to open and close doors for a young evangelist.

The word got around that Hershel Barnett was a rising star in the evangelistic circuit. Naturally, the church leaders were curious, so they came to see for themselves.

After a fantastic final service, Mom slipped across the street to the parsonage while Dad continued praying and talking with the people. There was no air conditioning in those days, so she opened her window to the warm Texas night and started to settle into sleep when faint, but familiar, voices filtered into her room. The district superintendent and the presbyter were talking about what they had witnessed that night and about the rising young evangelist.

"Well, what did you think about him?" the presbyter asked, alluding to young Hershel Barnett.

"He's a good preacher," the official noted. "I believe he can go far."

"But," interjected the presbyter, "what will he ever do with that wife of his? She can't even play the guitar or sing. She can't do anything. She will hurt his ministry."

Those cold, condemning words stabbed my mother's young and tender heart. She sobbed into the pillow, fearful that the leaders were right. She would be a drag on Hershel's ministry because she was so shy and "untalented." She felt she had been selfish in wanting Dad so much, and if he had only chosen a more gifted wife, he could reach his potential. The overheard conversation had shaken her to the soul, letting loose all the normal misgivings of a young bride. When my father came to bed, Mom pretended to be asleep so he would not know her hurt or see her crying.

Joy Barnett understood the ministry to which God had called her. She was also aware of her own inadequacies. She was in many ways like Moses when God spoke to him out of a burning bush. Moses was told about the promise to give them the land of Canaan and that he was going to be the one to deliver them.

Questions were running through Moses' mind: Who, me? Why me? I can't do it!

That's when God asked him, "What is that in your hand?"

Completely confused, Moses replied, "A staff," probably thinking to himself, The only thing I can deliver from Egypt with this is sheep (Ex. 4:2).

But the staff of Moses, a simple shepherd's stick, became the staff of God. With it Moses performed miracles before Pharaoh, turned the waters of the Nile into blood and brought forth frogs, gnats, locusts, thunder and hail upon the land of Egypt. He lifted up the staff and stretched it over the Red Sea, and it parted. He struck the rock at Meribah (see Ex. 17), and water flowed out.

God can take our limited abilities and use them for great purposes. The key is offering up those abilities, feeble as they may be, to God. Then that insignificant thing in our hand becomes the staff of God.

Mom did not sleep much that night. But when dawn came she had made a decision. She would not give up in defeat. She would not prove those men right. From the pain she felt, a righteous anger and determination rose. Like Moses she seemed to hear God say, "What is that in your hand?"

Joy Patten Barnett searched her soul and took inventory of her potentials. Although she was too shy to stand before an audience, she decided she could write scripts and produce pageants, plays and skits. She could design costumes, paint backdrops, organize drama. The ideas kept coming.

She would take music lessons. She would do everything she could to polish what little she had and become an asset to her husband rather than a liability.

It was as if God said to her, "Joy, what is that in your hand?" The first thing the two Old Testament widows had to do was recognize the miracle that was already in their houses. For Mom she had to recognize the staff in her hand.

Neither the widows' provisions, the staff of Moses nor Mom's talent amounted to much in themselves. But God's plan was to use what they had.

The pain of that warm Texas night changed and challenged my dear mother. She refused to cave in to the negative expectations of others and determined to be the very best. And, in my opinion, she became just that.

Mom developed into one of the most dynamic of pastors' wives, pioneering pageants and dramatic productions in churches. Her original plays were performed nationally, and she became a highly sought-after speaker. People came to her and called her from all over the world for her counsel.

Years later those who saw and knew my mother would have been shocked that anyone would have uttered such cruelties that painful night so long ago.

I am learning to make troubles my servant. I am also learning to see situations that challenge my ability as opportunities to see God empower my feeble efforts. God doesn't allow us to be tempted beyond that which we are able. Neither does He challenge us without supplying His help.

Look at what Paul learned through facing insurmountable obstacles with limited ability:

AND He has said to me, "My grace is sufficient for you, for power is perfected in weakness." Most gladly, therefore, I will rather boast about my weaknesses, that the power of Christ may dwell in me.

2 Corinthians 12:9

God often picks for a job a person who lacks the ability to accomplish it. One of the prerequisites of tapping into God's grace and power is the realization of your own inability. James wrote,

> BUT He gives a greater grace. Therefore it says, "God is opposed to the proud, but gives grace to the humble."
>
> James 4:6

We receive grace to accomplish great things through God's power in the same way we receive grace for salvation. In order to be saved, a person must first humble himself and admit that he has no ability to save himself. Then he receives the grace for salvation.

When you realize that by your ability you can't accomplish the task God has placed before you, you are only one step away from finding that through His power you can do all things. As we grow in faith we learn to look to God for His grace and not to our own abilities.

Many times God will use needs to show you both His power and part of His plan for your life. I often tell people, "If you don't know what to do, find the need and fill it. And if you don't think you have the ability, just trust God, use what you have and do what you can."

WE NEEDED SOMEONE TO work the wheelchair ministry. We had about thirty people to whom we were reaching out. Sharon Henning had been helping, so I asked her to take over for a few weeks until we found someone else. I was amazed to find that she started bringing twice as many people as we had before. Nevertheless, at the end of a few weeks she came to me and said, "I don't feel God's called me to this. Please hurry up and find someone else to take over."

I told her that I understood how she felt, but because the need was there and she was having such success, I wanted her to continue for a little while until I got someone.

That ministry grew to the point that on one Sunday at church she had four hundred people who were in wheelchairs or were disabled.

Finally she came to me and said, "Pastor, I've got to take that back. I feel that God has called me to do this."

Today Sharon Henning is a wonderful ambassador for Christ and one of the greatest Christian workers I have ever seen do anything. It began with a need, and she took what she had in her hand to meet it. Before that Sharon had not established any great ministry nor commanded a great following. She was not a dynamic speaker but simply had a heart for hurting people and a real love for God.

You can take a job nobody else wants and make it so great that they'll have to hire you because they won't be able to do without it. That's how most people came to be on my staff.

Now Sharon Henning is a part of our church's paid staff and has become the leading authority in the city — and maybe in the world — on reaching hurting people in wheelchairs. At our last Fourth of July rally she brought over eight hundred people to church. Even though she is scared to death to stand up and speak, Sharon receives invitations to speak from all over the nation.

Trouble can be a stumbling block, or it can become your servant and be a stepping stone. The same is true when you face insurmountable obstacles and feel totally inadequate. It is the chance of a lifetime. Whether they are forced upon you or you simply accept the challenge to meet a need, you'll discover how God can use the gifts and talents you possess when they are placed at His disposal. So troubles and need bring out the best in you, and when the best of you is brought out, you discover the special talent God has planted in you.

Most of us would jump at the chance to have a burning bush or Damascus road experience with God. But if you get that close to God, He might just say something like "Go and deliver My people from Pharaoh's hand" or "I have called you as an apostle to the gentiles."

God takes no account of your abilities or lack thereof. He only sees your possibilities. What He looks for is people who are willing to accept the challenge to meet the need.

When faced with desperate needs and overwhelming challenges, look to God and ask Him to help you see if the seed of your miracle is already in your hand. When you recognize it, offer it to God in faith that the works of God would be displayed through you.

FIVE

Finding the
Miracle Within

INSIDE EVERY human being is a miracle waiting to be discovered and released.

Pastors ask me over and over how I seem to be able to motivate and develop the potential in all the great people I serve. There are two simple answers to that question. First of all, I am convinced that every Christian has the innate desire to do something great for God, to lay down at the foot of the cross the biggest gift he or she possibly can. All the needed motivation already exists inside them.

Second, and most important, I believe in people. That is the key to leadership. I believe there's a special calling, purpose and gift waiting to be manifested through every person. As a pastor, one of my primary concerns is helping people discover the special measure of grace God has put in them.

We live in a society where kids are so often told that they can't do anything right, that they're no good and that they're not really wanted. I've had so many people tell me, "Pastor Tommy, you are the only person who has ever believed in me." Even when a person shows no outward signs of potential at all, I just believe it's there. Each person has a special grace and calling.

Of course, there are people who attend Phoenix First Assembly who at first have a hard time believing God can use them to do anything. Believing in yourself, however, can become contagious. These members see many people with no more ability than they have stepping out in faith, pouring into empty vessels and seeing miracles happen. As a result, they begin to believe they can do great things too.

Hundreds of Christian conferences are held each year in every part of the country. In order to get people to come, the biggest and the best speakers are invited and advertised. Each year we have more than six thousand pastors and church leaders attend a conference at our church. But we do little advertising, and we don't have any guest speakers. All the sessions and workshops are taught by our staff and laypeople.

So many keep coming each year because each person walks away with the idea that if these people can do it, certainly I can too. We have created an atmosphere that causes people to begin to believe in themselves. Now we're having to expand to two conferences a year.

WHEN PEOPLE FIND THEIR grace and calling, it's like striking oil. The searching process is sometimes long and hard, but the returns are overwhelming.

One of the best ways to discern the calling of God is to discover the special measure of grace which is your gift from God. Many people labor to fulfill some occupation or calling that is not theirs. Their ministry or occupation is a burden because the grace of God is not working with them. This often happens when people try to be what others expect of them. At other times people fail to discover their gifts because their priorities are wrong. They consider one calling more socially esteemed and are determined to do that, with or without the grace of God.

I have noticed that when people operate in their giftings, they feel a sense of power, grace and fulfillment. I used to have an old Plymouth. When I would crank it up on a cold morning, it would cough and sputter. I would start off to the church running on about five cylinders. Even with the accelerator pushed to the floor, the car would barely move. But when that old engine warmed up and all eight cylinders kicked in, I could feel a surge of power.

That's the way it feels when you serve in an area that uses the gifts God has given you. You feel the grace of God kick in. Sharon Henning found that grace and gifting when she reluctantly took over the wheelchair ministry.

It is no wonder that the Bible so often mentions grace and the calling of God together. In each of the following examples, Paul refers to his calling as an apostle or to the ministry gifts of Ephesians 4 as a function of the graces and abilities given by the Holy Spirit.

BUT to each one of us grace was given according to the measure of Christ's gift.
⁸Therefore it says,

"When He ascended on high,
He led captive a host of captives,
And He gave gifts to men."...

¹¹And He gave some as apostles, and some as

prophets, and some as evangelists, and some as pastors and teachers.

Ephesians 4:7-8,11

I was made a minister, according to the gift of God's grace which was given to me according to the working of His power.

⁸To me, the very least of all saints, this grace was given, to preach to the Gentiles the unfathomable riches of Christ.

Ephesians 3:7-8

THROUGH whom we [the apostles] have received grace and apostleship [the calling to be an apostle]....

Romans 1:5a

AND since we have gifts that differ according to the grace given to us, let each exercise them accordingly: if prophecy, according to the proportion of his faith;

⁷if service, in his serving; or he who teaches, in his teaching.

Romans 12:6-7

When you find yourself serving with the gifts and in the calling God has given you, the power of His grace becomes a reality. Grace is not just forgiveness and unmerited favor. Grace is God's strength and power enabling you to do more and be more than you ever could in your own strength. Listen to what the apostle Paul said about working with the help of grace.

BUT by the grace of God I am what I am, and His grace toward me did not prove vain; but I labored even more than all of them, yet not I, but the grace of God with me.

1 Corinthians 15:10

God has graced so many people in our church with ministries any of which would exhaust me in a very short period of time: Larry Kerychuk and his great ministry to college and professional athletes; Lloyd Zeigler and his tireless work leading the Master's Commission; Leo Godzich and his ministry to AIDS patients; Jeff Allaway and his persistence in inner-city bus ministry in over 100 degree temperatures; Lorna Gail, who selflessly directs ten ministries related to women; Diana Nutt, who directs the largest totally volunteer nursery and early childhood ministry that I know of; Walt Ratray, who ministers each week to over two thousand transients, homeless and prisoners with seven homes to house them in and a mission. The list goes on to include hundreds of deacons and deaconesses and over 180 ministries to the hurting.

Each of us has learned that when we work long and hard, we feel physically tired, but inside we feel invigorated because we are working in the calling and by the grace God has given.

Be Careful What You Do With That Gift

The word *burden* is often used by people to describe God's guidance and direction. "I've got the burden for China," says one, while "My burden is for Africa," says another.

What people mean by *burden* is that they feel a desire or compassion to help a certain group of people. I feel compassion for lots of people groups. Nevertheless, I am not led by my burden as much as I am by my calling. I have found burdens come and go, but the sense of calling remains. For example, I don't feel a great burden to get up at 5:00 A.M. to pray, but I feel called to it. So I'm up.

The word *burden* is found in its Hebrew and Greek forms throughout the Bible, but in almost every case it has a negative connotation, implying that a burden is something you don't want to have. The most notable reference in the New Testament is when Jesus said, "My yoke is easy, and my burden is light" (Matt. 11:30, KJV).

On several occasions in the Old Testament, a reference is made to the "burden of the word of the Lord," but in no case did the burden refer to the prophet's compassion for the people to whom he was called (see Zech. 9:1, 12:1; Mal. 1:1). It was more a sense of obligation to be faithful as God's messenger.

As I have said, each one of us has a special calling and gift of grace to use in serving the Lord. But just as there was the burden of the word of the Lord, there is the burden of the gift of God. In other words, we are stewards of our gifts and graces. What shall we do with what we have been given?

Notice how Peter understands our accountability as stewards for the grace we have received.

> As each one has received a special gift, employ it in serving one another, as good stewards of the manifold grace of God.
>
> 1 Peter 4:10

Listen to what the apostle Paul says:

> Indeed you have heard of the stewardship of God's grace which was given to me for you.
>
> Ephesians 3:2

Every person has a gift and measure of special grace, but many people never discover it because they are unwilling to let it operate. Others recognize the potential miracle within them, but if they never use it, they will never feel the power of God working in and through them. Even though the grace and potential existed, if the widow had not poured into the empty vessels, no miracle would have occurred.

In the parable of the talents, one of the servants took the talent he had been given and hid it because of his fear. The talent was taken from him and given to the one who had many. The parable ended with these words:

FOR to everyone who has shall more be given, and he shall have an abundance; but from the one who does not have, even what he does have shall be taken away.

Matthew 25:29

We have found that if we pour, we get more! What motivates us to serve is not the fear of judgment if we don't use our gifts, but the desire to feel the grace of God working through us. The greatest joy you can have in life is to find a gift of grace and use it to serve others. When you discover that, you want to serve more and more.

One man said to me, "Pastor, if you said we needed to provide a steak dinner for five thousand hurting, homeless people, the members of this church would drive a herd of steers right through the auditorium to try to provide that food."

Why do people respond so enthusiastically when I give them a chance to serve by pouring into empty vessels? They've learned that the greatest joy in living is giving.

See the Need and Take the Lead

Shortly after our bus ministry had fueled dramatic growth in the church, a jolly young man flew to Phoenix to meet with me.

"Pastor, I saw you on television the other day. You said the way to grow a church is to find a need and fill it. I heard you talk about how you started with one old bus, and as soon as it was filled you bought another and then another, until six months later you had forty buses."

He went on to tell me everything that I, of course, already knew: how one ministry after another had been started.

Then he said, "Pastor, there are over four hundred thousand senior citizens in Phoenix. Nobody is reaching them, but God has laid it on my heart to help you reach them. Pastor Barnett, if you'll hire me, I'll reach 'em."

My initial response almost made me miss the miracle God had for me. "I can't afford it," I said.

"Then I'll work for free," said Keith Buchanan.

Well, it was hard to pass on that deal. During the next several years, Keith became phenomenally successful and developed a great ministry. Because of Keith, I have found myself going to the board again and again, asking them to buy more buses.

The same is true in business. Tom Peters and Robert Waterman in their best-selling book *In Search of Excellence: Lessons From America's Best Run Companies* reveal that success in business comes from recognizing needs.

An engineer at 3M corporation sang in the choir at his church and needed a bookmark that would not fall out of his hymnal. He fooled around for months trying to solve his problem. As a result, today we have 3M's Post-it note pads, and those who work in offices feel they cannot do without them. Virtually without exception, the last few chairmen and all the key executives at 3M were people who recognized needs and championed products to meet those needs.[1]

Some people want to do something great for God, yet they have not responded to the needs He has placed before them. Whether in ministry or in business, success and position are not going to be handed to you. No one's preparing an invitation for you to be the head of a great ministry or the president of a big corporation.

Some people think if they just had a certain position, they could do great things. But the position won't make you great. You can take any job or any ministry and make it explode, if you will only find the need and meet it.

You will see a marvelous work in your life if you simply practice this principle. Don't worry about how to meet the need. Just step out in faith, and God will show you how. Find the need and take the lead!

Find Yourself: You're in There Somewhere

I don't like using the phrases "called into the ministry" or "called to preach." They seem to imply that ministry or preaching is some kind of special position for only a selected few. We are all called in one way or another to be ministers of Jesus Christ and to tell others about the good news.

You are not an accidental person. God has a unique purpose for you that only you can fulfill. No one else can do it, and if you don't fulfill that purpose, no one else will.

Of course there may be someone else who will take that job, marry that man or share the gospel with that hurting person. But even if someone does replace you, he or she will neither be able nor inclined to carry out that purpose in the same way you would have done it.

I have a wife and three children, and each one of them loves me differently. Each one encourages me, challenges me and delights me in a special way that no one else in the world can.

If you don't praise God and love Him, someone else will. But not exactly as you would.

God has a task on which He desires to see your special touch. Others could do it, but not with your unique touch.

YEARS AGO IN A little Southern town a man was carving a bust out of a large piece of wood. Eventually that log became a statue of Abraham Lincoln. One little boy who had seen the beginning of the project looked in amazement at the figure and said, "Wow, I didn't know Abraham Lincoln was in that log!" Yes, Lincoln was in there all along. He just had not been discovered.

A lot of people are like the prophet Jeremiah, needing to discover who they are.

> NOW the word of the Lord came to me saying,
>
> 5"Before I formed you in the womb I
>   knew you,
> And before you were born I consecrated
>   you;
> I have appointed you a prophet to the
>   nations."
>
> Jeremiah 1:4-5

God revealed to Jeremiah that his life-purpose was to be the prophet to the nation. That had been determined even before Jeremiah had been conceived in the womb.

From birth, Jeremiah was who God had made him to be. Now it was time for Jeremiah to find out who he really was, to discover who he had always been.

Each one of you was made with a special purpose in mind. You're a lot like that log with the bust of Lincoln in it. Somewhere in there is the real you. It's up to you to make the discovery.

I have often said that on a Wednesday night over forty years ago at Victoria Tabernacle in Kansas City, Missouri, I was called to preach. It is more accurate, I am now sure, to say that on that night I simply found myself. I realized who I was and what I was meant to be. I found that inside that little boy was a preacher. And once I realized who I was, things that were not truly who I was began to fall away.

You see, the devil's plan for you is to make you into someone or something that you're not. He wants to distort your understanding of who you are. To create the statue, the woodcarver simply needed to chip away the things that didn't look like Lincoln. That's the last thing Satan wants us to do — allow God to chip away the excess in our lives and reveal who we are and His plan and purpose for us. So the more sin we can be tempted to live with, the less likely we are to discover who we really are and what God's purpose for our lives is.

You should not think of the two paths before you as God's plan or the devil's plan. The choice is between who you are and who you are not.

People who are living in sin and selfishness are lost — lost in the sense that they haven't yet found themselves. The literal definition of the Greek word for *sin* is "to miss the mark."[2] To live in sin is to be walking down the wrong road on the way to being someone you are not.

Even before you were in your mother's womb, God consecrated you — that is, set you apart — to do and be something for Him. The real joy, peace and fulfillment are in being who you are.

You're in there somewhere. Find yourself!

SIX

How Many Loaves Do You Have?

WHEN I arrived in Phoenix, two hundred people were meeting every Sunday in a twelve-hundred-seat auditorium. To say the least, nobody was crowded in the pews.

After ten months fifteen hundred were attending, and we had gone to two Sunday morning services. That's significant growth by any standard, but I still felt that the church needed something to get it off dead center. This had been a church that spent most of its time reaching inward to feed itself.

With the Thanksgiving holidays approaching, I stood before the church on Sunday morning and announced, "We're going to do what Jesus did. We're going to feed five thousand people. I want you all to come tonight, and I'm going to tell you how it is going to happen."

One of the new converts met me on the way out of church and asked, "Pastor Tommy, where are you going to get all of that food?"

"Well," I said, "I'm going to take a few loaves and a few fishes. I'm going to pray over them and break them, and we're going to feed the multitude."

With wide eyes the young convert said, "Wow, are you really going to do it that way, pastor?"

"No, not literally," I had to explain quickly, "but you come tonight, and you're going to see a miracle."

A GREAT MULTITUDE FOLLOWED Jesus as He went far away from the city seeking a remote and secluded place to rest. He taught many things to those who had come so far with Him. But at the end of the day the disciples were telling Jesus that something needed to be done about all these people and their need for food.

BUT He answered and said to them, "You give them something to eat!" And they said to Him, "Shall we go and spend two hundred denarii on bread and give them something to eat?"

^{38}And He said to them, "How many loaves do you have? Go look!" And when they found out, they said, "Five and two fish."

^{39}And He commanded them all to recline by groups on the green grass.

^{40}And they reclined in companies of hundreds and of fifties.

^{41}And He took the five loaves and the two fish, and looking up toward heaven, He blessed the

food and broke the loaves and He kept giving
them to the disciples to set before them; and He
divided up the two fish among them all.

⁴²And they all ate and were satisfied.

⁴³And they picked up twelve full baskets of the
broken pieces, and also of the fish.

⁴⁴And there were five thousand men who ate
the loaves.

Mark 6:37-44

ALMOST EVERYBODY CAME TO church that night. I
told them we wanted to feed everybody as Jesus had, but
in our case the menu would be turkey, dressing and all
the trimmings — everything we needed to feed the multitude, and we would do it free of charge.

"We'll need 160 people to bring baked turkeys, sliced
and prepared and ready to serve, and have them in the
kitchen by 6:00 A.M." One hundred and sixty stood. We did
the same for the ham, dressing, desserts and so on.

Then I said, "The Bible says that when you have a
feast, you don't just bring those who are full. You bring
those who are hungry. Where can we go to get these people?"

Different ones began to suggest that we go to the wel-
fare lines, food kitchens, orphanages and convalescent
homes. So we had our plan. We would invite our guests to
a Sunday morning service and feed them in the afternoon.

Sunday morning came. When I walked into the 8:00 A.M.
service, a smell hit me that I had never encountered at
Phoenix First Assembly. But it was not the smell of turkey. It was the stench of dirty humanity.

The auditorium was jam-packed that morning. The bal-
cony was crowded with four to five hundred of the dirti-
est, filthiest people I had ever seen. They had their
backpacks and bed rolls with them. Some of them even
brought their dogs.

I could just hear some of the class-conscious members of our church saying, "Since Barnett's been here, the church has gone to the dogs."

That morning I preached on how the King has paved the way back with love. I told them the food that day was prepared with love, the buses ran with love, and the way back to God was paved with love. There was a tremendous response.

I was amazed by the visitors in our church that morning. I had never seen people who were dirtier. The regular church attenders were in shock, too. Some would consider these to be the scourge and plague of the city but not God. And the next service had so many people that they couldn't get them in.

I didn't realize it but right around our church the parks were full of transients who had come to Arizona for the winter. Our people had gone out and invited the transients, and they had overrun the church that day.

Since we couldn't get them all in, I sent many of the men into the parking lots to preach to the people in small groups. Then they went through the food line. There were sixty-seven hundred people in church that day.

It became such an event that it made the front page of the local newspaper. Soon after seeing what a tremendous thing had happened, some other churches got together and decided they were going to have the world's greatest Feed-the-Multitude Sunday. The dinner would be so big that it would be put in the *Guinness Book of World Records*.

They rented a football field and got all the major hotels to donate chefs, food and equipment. That Thanksgiving the local media gave all the publicity to the Feed-the-Multitude Sunday, which was OK with us. We still fed our ill-smelling mob.

But they ended up having only about three thousand people. Why? They were trying to feed the people that had already been fed, while we were feeding empty vessels. They ended up giving us their food.

We've kept on feeding the multitudes every year since then. At our last Thanksgiving dinner we had over seventeen thousand people feast on the meal and hear about the love of Jesus Christ. Every year we have more than we need. The church members bring so much. We take all the leftovers to soup kitchens. Those who get the meal appreciate it, but it is the church that always gets the biggest blessing.

IN THE NEXT TEN years there is going to be an abundance of needy people in our society — and not just with financial needs. There will be divorce; broken homes; incurable diseases like AIDS; all kinds of abuse, addictions and emotional problems; a growing number of older people who need help; and many with a general emptiness from not knowing Jesus Christ as their Savior. What a great time and a great opportunity for the church. That's our mission — to show the love, grace and power of Jesus to a hurting world.

However, some look at the growing critical needs and conclude that they are more than the church can handle. The church says we don't have enough to feed the multitude of problems.

But that's not so. We have all we need already, and it's in our house. The church has all the resources it needs to show the love of Christ to the world, and those resources are already sitting in the pews. Maybe there aren't many sitting in the pews in some places, but if those who are there begin to pour, God will miraculously multiply your pouring and your pourers.

We were instructed to pray for God to send laborers, but it is our responsibility to compel the hungry guests to come in. It was the widow's responsibility to gather the empty vessels, and it was the Lord who multiplied what she had to pour into them.

When faced with an overwhelming need and a limited

supply, the disciples went to Jesus and recommended He do something. Their suggestion was to send the hungry crowd away. Their needs were too great. Jesus' response to them was "You give them something to eat!"

How could they? There were only twelve of them. Jesus continued: "How many loaves do you have? Go look!" All they could find was a little lunch, and that was borrowed. What good would that do when the needs were so great?

Constantly people talk to me about "what the church ought to do."

"But there's nothing more I can do," I say to them. And like Jesus I frequently tell them, "*You* do something!" or "*You* give them something to eat." Many times they have accepted the challenge and offered what little they had, and the miracle of multiplication occurred. That's how all those ministries in our church began.

One night we were to have a communion service. As is our custom on those occasions, spotlights shone on only the front of the church while the houselights were dimmed. After the elements had been distributed, I said as I usually do, "Has everyone been served?"

I had prearranged for three or four people to respond to my question. The first one stood and said, "Pastor Barnett, the people who live in the park — they have not been served."

Then someone from the wheelchair ministry said, "There are those hurting people in wheelchairs; they have not been served."

After the few I had prearranged stood and spoke, others in the congregation began to stand and identify those who had not been served.

Several new ministries were birthed that night out of the realization that hurting people were out there who had not been served by the church. Some of these ministries are highlighted in a later chapter.

Ellen Dodge stood and said the victims of crime were not being served. I really didn't think there would be many people in that category. So I asked the congregation, "How many of you have been a victim of crime in the last year?" Over half of the people raised their hands. A large segment of our society has been victimized, and it leaves a mark on them.

Today Ellen has a ministry to victims of crime and to those who have suffered great losses. She sends out letters to people who have been in serious accidents, to those who are getting divorces or dealing with a death in the family. We check the newspapers for those who have been through tragedies, and we let them know we feel for their hurts and would like to do anything we can to help.

Are there people in your community who have not been served? Go and see what you have, even if it seems insignificant, and then give them something. That's how miracles begin.

IS THERE ANYONE OUT there who feels as if he has dried up as a Christian? Is there anyone who has lost the joy of salvation and whose worship has become rote? Are there people who feel deep in their hearts that they are slipping away from God and realize they have become at best only lukewarm Christians but don't know how to be hot again?

Yes, there are millions.

Keith Green had the ability to express both the heart of God and the heart of people in song. He wrote:

> My eyes are dry, my faith is old.
> My heart is hard, my prayers are cold.
> And I know how I ought to be,
> Alive to You and dead to me.
> Oh, what can be done for an old heart like mine,
> Soften it up with oil and wine.
> The oil is You, Your Spirit of love.
> Please wash me anew in the wine of Your blood.[1]

If this description fits you, don't feel condemned. The world we live in exerts a constant downward pull on every Christian. And we all to one degree or another have the same problem. Paul wrote in his letter to the Corinthians that these temptations were common to all people but that certainly God would provide a way of escape for us (1 Cor. 10:13).

The most discouraging part for some is the thought that having lost their first love, they can never find it again. But the Scripture passage doesn't say they "lost" their first love. It says they "left" their first love (Rev. 2:4). When you lose things, sometimes they can never be found again. If you've left something, you can always go back for it — that is, if you can just remember the way.

As Christians we all long to have the abundant life that Jesus talked about flowing constantly out of us. Jesus explained this abundant life to a Samaritan woman at a well where she was drawing water. John records His conversation with her:

EVERYONE who drinks of this water shall thirst again;
    [14]but whoever drinks of the water that I shall give him shall never thirst; but the water that I shall give him shall become in him a well of water springing up to eternal life.
                                                    John 4:13-14

Sounds great, right? But where is it in my life? you may ask. If you have put your faith in the blood of Christ which was shed on the cross for your sins and have accepted Jesus Christ as your Savior, the Holy Spirit has come to live inside you. He is that living water that springs up. That's good news because you don't have to look anywhere but inside to find the source of your spiritual renewal.

If the well has ceased to flow, it's not because the living

water has run out. It's only that the well is clogged, and you need to clean out the pipes.

Many factors can cause spiritual dryness — more than we can talk about here. But there are a few simple overriding principles of the kingdom that, when discovered and acted upon, will enable you to deal effectively with many of the other problems.

I know this is not a new concept. It's simple, it's central to kingdom living, and it is essential to keeping the living waters flowing. It is, however, contrary to our natural way of thinking. Jesus expressed this principle in several different ways:

- If you want to live, you must die (Matt. 10:39).

- If you want to be great, become the servant of all (Matt. 23:11).

- If you want to be exalted, humble yourself (Matt. 23:12).

- It is more blessed to give than to receive (Acts 20:35).

A few chapters later John records more of Jesus' teaching about that living water.

IF any man is thirsty, let him come to Me and drink.
[38]He who believes in Me, as the Scripture said, "From his innermost being shall flow rivers of living water."

John 7:37-38

Take one drink, and it becomes a well! That's miracle talk. The miracle of the widow and the empty vessels caused the widow's oil to flow as long as she kept pouring. It is the lack of pouring that clogs the well. When you save your life instead of losing it, hoard instead of giving, expect service instead of serving, the oil of joy in your life dries up.

The remedy for your dryness? Start to serve and start to give. Find some empty vessels and start to pour. You may think that you have so little to give and that you must save that for yourself and your family. The widow at Zarephath faced the same situation. She had only enough for her son and herself to prepare their last meal and die. But she gave in faith, and the miracle occurred in her house.

Take a step of faith. Find some empty vessels and begin to pour. Perhaps you will discover why the well has been clogged all along. You will discover that there's a miracle in your house too — it's a well that won't run dry.

SEVEN

Miracles on
My Doorstep

I HAD come to preach a crusade in a city that sits like a running sore on the bloated underbelly of India. It was this experience that took the blinders off my eyes and enabled me to see the incredible miracles that were sitting right at my doorstep. In the years that followed, God has used and multiplied these "miracles in waiting." Much of the success in Phoenix began in Calcutta, India.

It was there I met the famous missionary Mark Buntain, one of the great saints of this century. He had gone to Calcutta years before and had singlehandedly turned on a light on what some call the front porch of hell. Books, movies and documentaries have been written about his remarkable work. He built hospitals, schools and churches and fed hundreds of thousands of starving people.

Only Mother Teresa has received more accolades and recognition than this great missionary who literally created an island of hope in a sea of despair. Even though Mark has now been graduated to heaven, his great work continues to touch tens of thousands of Indians every day in that lost land.

That night thousands of hungry, hurting Indians poured into the public racetrack to hear me preach. Mark Buntain had arranged the meeting, and as the crowds came in wearing their baggy, dirty wraps, my heart broke. Their dark eyes were like circles of black fire boring silently into me, pleading for help. I tried to let them know there was a God who loved them and would give them life even here.

While many precious Indians responded to the altar call, I did not feel the meeting was much of a success. Perhaps I was too emotionally moved by the horror of what I had seen around me. Maybe I was in culture shock. One thing was for sure: What I had witnessed would haunt me forever, and I would lie awake many nights weeping for their great sorrow.

As my plane swept down the runway and rose high over the sordid city of Calcutta, part of me was left there forever. I had not changed the city much, but it had changed me.

Winging away from that sorrowful city I determined the poor and powerless of our world deserve better than what they now know. I determined to do all I could to help them break the awful, gripping, grinding cycle of poverty and pain. I would help them find life through the Life-Giver.

As the years passed, the memories of those Calcutta scenes faded. But in Phoenix God again gave me a firsthand vision of His love and concern for hurting people, and all the memories of Calcutta returned. I determined again to give myself to those who had no one else to care. Like Isaiah I had heard God ask:

> WHOM shall I send as a messenger to my people? Who will go?"
> And I said, "Lord, I'll go! Send me."
>
> Isaiah 6:8, TLB

Many times when people come to the place of saying, "God, I'll go wherever You send me," they usually think of some place like Calcutta. I was willing to go, but for me the job began at home.

At the beginning I only thought that God's purpose was for me to meet the needs of hurting people. As time went on I realized that God was not just sending me to the poor; He was sending the poor to me to meet my needs. They were to become the answer to my prayers — just as it was with King David.

> SO David departed from there and escaped to the cave of Adullam; and when his brothers and all his father's household heard of it, they went down there to him.
> 2And everyone who was in distress, and everyone who was in debt, and everyone who was discontented, gathered to him; and he became captain over them. Now there were about four hundred men with him.
>
> 1 Samuel 22:1-2

Assembling an Army of Ragtags

Caring for the poor and powerless was neither new nor strange to me. I had seen my dad live out this passion. Although he had many church buses, he always also used his own car to pick up the poor to bring them to church.

Every Sunday after services our family waited at the church while Dad delivered his many riders back home. I once asked him why he did this, and he replied, "Son, I will never ask my people to do something that I will not do. This is our ministry. This is our calling."

People often laughed at my dad saying all he had in his church was a bunch of poor bus kids. But those poor bus kids grew up, and they never forgot the love my dad had shown.

When my dad died, the church was filled with people from all walks of life. Senator Bob Dole, the mayor of the city, city council members, prominent businesspeople and social leaders were all there. Hershel Barnett pastored Victoria Tabernacle in Kansas City for forty years, and during that time it became one of the largest churches in the denomination.

I stood at the head of my dad's casket and watched the people pass by to pay their final respects. Along with the high and mighty, an old, tattered street alcoholic brought his little, ragged mongrel dog to say good-bye.

Almost daily my dad would stop and talk to this street dweller, often giving him a little money and a piece of candy for his dog. Before the undertaker could stop him, the teary-eyed old alcoholic patted my dad, mumbling words of appreciation because this preacher had always treated him with respect regardless of how others had viewed him. Clutching his little dog, he leaned over the casket for a last look. The little mutt lovingly licked my dad on the nose. This was "their" pastor.

Some of the poor bus kids my dad reached out to developed into wonderful pastors and prominent leaders, great pastors like Bill Baker and Ray Thomas who had come to dad's church on the buses from families who never attended church. They were not just bus kids. They were miracles in the house.

ELISHA TOLD THE WIDOW to go out and bring back as many pots as she could. As she began to pour what little oil she had into empty vessels, the miracle occurred.

The greatest revival is always among empty vessels. Those who consider themselves to be filled don't thirst for more. In most churches Christians spend too much time filling themselves. We must be careful not to become addicted to the self-gratification of our senses when there are so many empty vessels waiting to be filled.

In our church the greatest miracles are taking place among street people, bikers, drug addicts and prison inmates. Revival is where the hurting people are.

Jesus told a story about a man who was giving a big dinner. He invited many people, but most were preoccupied with other things. The man finally said to his servant:

> GO out at once into the streets and lanes of the city and bring in here the poor and crippled and blind and lame."
> [22]And the slave said, "Master, what you commanded has been done, and still there is room."
> [23]And the master said to the slave, "Go out into the highways and along the hedges, and compel them to come in, that my house may be filled."
> Luke 14:21-23

People without a need won't come to the feast. They're not hungry.

I WAS WORRYING THAT our church ministry was getting a little stale. We had at that time eighty outreach ministries, but I knew there were more empty vessels to fill. We needed to find them. I remembered that when the widow had no more vessels to fill, the miracle was over.

So I asked the church one night, "What else can we do?"

One by one people stood up. One lady said, "We need to start a ministry to reach prostitutes. I used to be a prostitute, and no one is doing anything to help them."

I then said to her, "I now make you the head of the prostitute ministry."

Another stood, "Only Salt Lake City has a larger Mormon population than Phoenix."

"I now make you the head of the Mormon ministry."

And that man started a church within our church to reach out to Mormons.

"We have a city full of Jews," another said.

"I now put you in charge of the ministry to the Jews."

Gene Johnson stood and said, "What about young girls who have gotten pregnant and don't want to abort their babies?"

Gene and Carolyn opened their home to some young unwed mothers. Soon it was filled with young girls. However, the man who owned the house next door didn't approve of what they were doing. So when the house was available, they rented it and filled it with empty vessels, and the ministry has continued ever since. Today the Johnsons have a dynamic ministry of pouring into teenage girls, and miracles are happening in their lives.

"I think we need to do something for the throwaway kids," one young man said — and he did it. He took in the little throwaway kids on his bus route until he had a total of thirty-four living in his home over a period of several years.

This meeting came during the time when the AIDS epidemic was first getting national attention. In those days when much less was known about how the disease could and could not be spread, Leo Godzich stood and said, "Pastor Tommy, we've got to do something for the victims of AIDS." Today Leo has led more than a hundred AIDS patients to the Lord and is a national spokesperson to churches on reaching out to these people with such great needs.

After the service was over, Mike Weymouth came up to me and said, "Pastor, I think God has called me to reach out to the motorcycle people. I used to ride with that bunch, and they need to hear about Jesus Christ."

So Mike became the leader of our new motorcycle

church. Of course, it had no members — at least not yet. Mike used to be a drug dealer before he became a Christian. At first he was very apprehensive about knocking on doors. But he decided he would put away his hesitations and trust God to take care of all that. It's not that Mike was ashamed of Christ. He just knew that behind one of those doors might be someone out to kill him over a past drug deal.

I was totally in support of all these new ministries to hurting people. But the motorcycle church worried me a little. I'm a pretty straight guy and not used to people in black leather, chains and tattoos. Who knew what kinds of weapons they were carrying with them? I had to enlarge my circle of love to include them too.

I will never forget the first time I saw them come into the parking lot. Their Harleys were popping as they rolled in like Hell's Angels. Oh no, I thought, what will the deacons say? The church members had been careful to remind me that Phoenix is a white-collar city.

We bought a bar on the edge of our property and started the Church in the Wind. Ten months later more than three hundred bikers were filling it every Sunday morning. Now Mike has to have two services. We are currently looking to buy or build a large metal building with air conditioning, a concrete floor and a large door. That way they can drive right into church on their bikes and bring all their biker friends with them. Mike will have a world-class, drive-in motorcycle church.

Pork Chop was a four-hundred-pound biker whom Mike led to Christ. He was well-known to motorcycle people and became a dedicated missionary to his old friends. One day, while on an outreach, Pork Chop had a heart attack and died. Mike was right there, giving CPR and mouth-to-mouth resuscitation.

Mike Weymouth's dedication to Christ and his love for these people are becoming legendary. Every week more bikers are getting saved, and they follow Mike as if he were the Pied Piper.

Why? Because he was willing to pour himself into empty vessels.

WALT RATRAY CAME TO me from another church during the first year I was in Phoenix. His previous church had asked him to leave because he kept bringing so many street people to their meetings.

"The other church didn't want me," Walt said. "Do you?"

"Walt, I want you more than anything in the world" was my reply. "I not only *want* you; I *need* you!"

I told Walt he could use one of our buses, and on the first Wednesday night he brought a bus load of street people into that very class-conscious church. One man who came with Walt had had a little too much to drink. Before I even got into the service, this man was in the pulpit, wanting to preach. As he was being escorted back to his seat, I came into the meeting and ran right into Walt.

"Oh, pastor, I'm so sorry. I won't bring any more if you don't want me to."

"I want you to bring even more next week," I told Walt. And he did.

We didn't let that stop us. The Church on the Street, as we started calling it, increased to the point that he was bringing five bus loads to church.

One of these was Richard Hudalla, who was found drunk on a cot in a shelter. Every week Walt would invite him to come to church, but he was always too drunk. All he gave were promises until one day Walt caught him when he was sober, and he came. Richard had been a very successful accountant before his life was destroyed by alcohol. He came to the altar, was saved and instantly delivered from alcohol and cigarettes. Now Richard is again a respected businessman and has a beautiful family. He is the business manager of the Church on the Street and Walt's right-hand man.

For a long time Walt's dream was to have his own church for these people with a home to put them in. Today he has the church, a mission and seven homes. Walt Ratray runs perhaps the nation's greatest outreach to street people.

Last week the Church on the Street reached out to twenty-five hundred hurting and homeless people. So many people are getting saved in the prisons that in one the officials even let us put in a baptismal tank.

One section of our church is filled with two hundred people from the park every Sunday evening. After church we feed them and provide them with showers, haircuts and new clothes.

Sunday afternoon the buses leave about 4:30 and go wherever they can find empty vessels — apartment houses, the battered women's home, shelters and so on. We pick up anyone who will come.

Every Sunday night many are led to Christ. Why? Because they are empty vessels. The revival is where people feel they have a need.

FRED BOULINEAU, AN EXECUTIVE for the Marriott corporation, agreed to be a part of our bus ministry. The first week that he drove a bus route he came back without picking up anyone. I knew that his bus route was in a Spanish-speaking neighborhood, and he didn't know a word of Spanish.

"Why don't you try a different route next week, Fred?" I asked him. "An English-speaking neighborhood would be less difficult."

"No, I am not going to accept defeat," he replied.

Fred went home and created a Spanish tract. He went out on the route with the tract, showed it to the people and invited them to come to church on Sunday night.

Last year more than six hundred people were saved through his bus ministry. He is believing God to double that number this year and is well on his way to reaching his goal of twelve hundred.

WHEN WE CARE FOR the poor and powerless God

blesses us with the prominent and powerful. I've heard it said many times by so-called experts that if you spend too much time reaching out to lower-class people, the middle and upper classes will never come. I never believed that, and I never will. The New Testament church had all kinds of people: Palestinian Jews, Hellenistic Jews from all over the Roman Empire, Galilean fishermen, Pharisaical scholars, rich, poor. Everyone was there, and they were in one accord and had all things in common. I don't know of a church that has more upper-class, successful people than Phoenix First Assembly. Pro athletes, movie stars, city officials and Fortune 500 CEOs are regularly in our church.

When we love those God loves, He gives us an abundance that others will never know. For example, I think of former United States senator Roger Jepsen. He had come to our Davenport, Iowa, church where he accepted Christ as his personal Savior and went on to become a powerful leader in Washington, D.C., for many years. His wife became a famed leader of women during the Reagan years, and they were faithful members of our church. Because we cared for the poor and powerless in Davenport, God gave us much more.

Mighty Messes to Mighty Men

David's mighty men started out as poor, disgruntled refugees (1 Sam. 22:2). But David wasn't doing them a favor by giving them a chance to join his army. They were his only hope.

God didn't send me to help the hurting. He sent the hurting to help me.

My church in Phoenix is filled with wonderful, respectable, successful and dedicated people. But many of them first came to church as drug addicts, street people or bikers.

One woman came to our church and sat on the front row for many months. She didn't attract much attention until someone saw her going into the men's rest room. She — or rather, he — was actually a man dressed up like a woman. He was a broken and distressed individual looking for help. Leo Godzich, who is in charge of our AIDS ministry and who had some understanding of his situation, ministered to him.

This man was saved and over time experienced a tremendous and thorough emotional healing. Today that man, who came dressed as a woman and was one week away from having a sex-change operation, serves alongside me as a visitation deacon in our church and is committed to the cause of Christ!

THE BRAVERY AND DEDICATION with which David was served by his mighty men are unparalleled. The men's loyalty went beyond obedience to commands. They were intensely devoted to him as friends.

THEN three of the thirty chief men went down and came to David in the harvest time to the cave of Adullam, while the troop of the Philistines was camping in the valley of Rephaim.

14And David was then in the stronghold, while the garrison of the Philistines was then in Bethlehem.

15And David had a craving and said, "Oh that someone would give me water to drink from the well of Bethlehem which is by the gate!"

16So the three mighty men broke through the camp of the Philistines, and drew water from the well of Bethlehem which was by the gate, and took it and brought it to David. Nevertheless he would not drink it, but poured it out to the Lord;

17and he said, "Be it far from me, O Lord, that I should do this. Shall I drink the blood of the men who went in jeopardy of their lives?" Therefore he would not drink it. These things the three mighty men did.

2 Samuel 23:13-17

I could never say enough about the mighty men and women whom God has put around me. They protect me, they encourage me, and they never cease to amaze me. I haven't done so much for them. I only believe in them, that each one has the seeds for greatness within. People say, "Look at what a church Tommy Barnett has built." But other men and women did it. I was just a cheerleader. I just believed in people.

Jesus believed in people, too. He placed the proclamation of the good news in the hands of twelve men. If they had failed, the gospel would not have gotten out!

In 1971 God sent a young couple, Dale and Lynn Lane, to my church in Davenport, Iowa. They had a heart to serve God. Their lives were challenged. They devoted themselves, their time, their family and their finances to the work of God.

Dale started as a bus driver but was always looking for greater needs to fill. Early one very cold winter morning, I was trying to start the engines of the fleet of buses (not an easy thing to do at that time of year). I was getting very frustrated. Dale stepped in and said, "Pastor, go study and prepare for preaching. You don't need to be out here. From now on, I will come early every Sunday morning and make sure they are all started."

It was about that same time that Lynn became my secretary. She devoted her life to serving. Her good spirit, faithfulness, dedication, skills and attention to details have literally added years to my life.

Dale is now my associate pastor, and I believe he is the most noted associate in America. I consider him my "Aaron." He is my arms, my legs, my hands extended. I can always count on him. We are of like heart and like mind, both devoted to winning souls and meeting needs.

You see, in the early years I poured my life into Dale and Lynn. Now they live their lives pouring back into not only Phoenix First Assembly, but into people all over America. They could be building a great church themselves anywhere in America, but I am glad they felt more could be accomplished for God by working as a team with me and the staff of our church.

IT WAS A FEW months before Marja and I were to celebrate my fortieth anniversary in the ministry when I got wind of their plan. At first I thought it was a joke, but then I realized they were serious. These people were going to rent out the America West Arena where the Phoenix Suns play basketball, have people fly in from all over the country and put on the biggest anniversary party anyone had ever seen.

They were inviting celebrities, sports figures, politicians and so on. People from Davenport and individuals who were saved when I was in evangelistic ministry were coming, as well as a long list of pastors whose lives and ministries had been touched at our annual pastors' school. It was to be the grandest of all pastors' anniversary celebrations.

No one was risking his life for this project, but I did feel a little bit like David in the cave of Adullam. He couldn't accept the gift, and neither could we. Marja and I put a stop to it. It didn't matter so much to us whether or not we had that great party. What really mattered was that they wanted to do it.

If I have learned anything in Phoenix, it is this: If you pour into empty vessels when you are feeling empty yourself, they'll pour much more back into you.

The Shoes of Happiness

Famed preacher-poet Edwin Markham captured the essence of Christlike living and giving in relating the story of Conrad the Cobbler. In his classic work "The Shoes of

Happiness," Markham states that saintly Conrad had a
vivid dream in which he was told Christ would visit his
humble cobbler shop on a certain day.[1] The dream was so
real that Conrad was certain Jesus would indeed come.
So he decorated his simple shop with boughs of green and
prepared breads and cakes to serve the Master.

Early on the morning that Jesus was to visit, two of
Conrad's friends came by, and Conrad shared the dramatic dream with them. They wanted to wait for the Master with him because they knew that if anyone in the
village would ever have a visit from Jesus it would be
kindly Conrad. However, Conrad told them the Lord had
said specifically that He wanted to visit with the cobbler
alone. Markham wrote:

> His friends went home; and his face grew still
> As he watched for the shadow across the sill;
> He lived all the moments o'er and o'er,
> When the Lord should enter the lowly door.
> The knock, the call, the latch pulled up,
> The lighted face, the offered cup.
> He would wash the feet where the spikes had been;
> He would kiss the hands where the nails went in;
> And then at last he would sit with Him
> And break the bread as the day grew dim.

But the Master did not come. Instead a beggar
knocked on the door and asked for a pair of shoes. Conrad was irritated by the interruption, but his kindly
heart would not let him ignore the need of the old man.
He hurriedly made the shoes and gave them to the poor
beggar, rushing him off so he would not interrupt or pre-
vent the visit of the Great Guest.

A little later another knock sounded, and Conrad was
sure this was the Master. But it was only a hungry old
woman carrying a heavy load of sticks. She asked for food,
which Conrad reluctantly gave her. The only food he had

89

was what he had prepared for the Master. With each bite Conrad's heart sank. He feared he would have nothing left for his Lord, and he secretly hoped she would leave a little. However, she devoured every crumb. Then the old woman asked if Conrad would help her to the edge of the village because her load was so heavy. He did not want to leave the shop, but again the cobbler could not turn down the frail old woman. He wrote a hasty note and put it on the door, hoping the Master would not miss it and leave. When Conrad returned, the note was still there, undisturbed, so he knew the Master had not yet come.

Late in the evening there was a final knock on the cobbler's door. Conrad's heart leapt within him, knowing at last this would be the Master. But when he opened the door he found a lost and crying child.

"Mister, I'm lost," the little lad cried. "Will you please help me find my home?"

Conrad sighed, gathered the little tot in his arms, retrieved his note from the wastebasket and again placed it on his shop door. He took the lost lad far across the village to his worried mother. Rushing back, he hoped he had not missed the Master and then saw the well-used note still unmoved. Conrad knew Jesus had not yet made His visit.

As the midnight hour approached Conrad knew now the Master would not appear at his door. It really had only been a dream.

The kind cobbler's heart was broken, and in his crushing sadness Conrad fell to his knees crying:

"Why is it, Lord, that your feet delay?
"Did you forget that this was the day?"
Then, soft in the silence, a voice he heard:
"Lift up your heart, for I have kept my word.
"Three times I came to your friendly door;
"Three times my shadow was on your floor.
"I was the beggar with the bruised feet;

"I was the woman you gave to eat;
"I was the child on the homeless street."

Poet Markham caught the passion of our Lord for the poor. Jesus says:

FOR I was hungry, and you gave Me something to eat; I was thirsty, and you gave Me drink; I was a stranger, and you invited Me in;
    [36]"naked, and you clothed Me; I was sick, and you visited Me; I was in prison, and you came to Me."
    [37]Then the righteous will answer Him, saying, "Lord, when did we see You hungry, and feed You, or thirsty, and give You drink?
    [38]"And when did we see You a stranger, and invite You in, or naked, and clothe You?
    [39]"And when did we see You sick, or in prison, and come to You?"
    [40]And the King will answer and say to them, "Truly I say to you, to the extent that you did it to one of these brothers of Mine, even the least of them, you did it to Me."

Matthew 25:35-40

God's Word demands we see the poor as people rather than cold statistics or despised parasites of society. Clearly, God insists that a person's worth has nothing to do with what he does or does not possess.

I have found that as we reach out to hurting people and continue to pour into empty vessels, the miracle God has been working in our midst continues. The fresh oil keeps multiplying, and the hurting people become the miracle in the house.

EIGHT

Don't Let Troubles Keep You From the Making of a Miracle

THE TOWN tore me apart! Front-page news stories, harsh editorials, caustic radio commentators and blistering editorial cartoons all threw their best punches, knocking me to my knees.

There was a lot at stake — really more than I realized. But I knew there was a miracle to be found in every situation. I just had to be careful not to let my troubles cause me to miss it. I see now that if I had responded according to my feelings, the blessing would have passed me by, and I would have lost the miracle.

I felt somewhat alone in the midst of the battle. Have you ever noticed that when you get in big trouble, people shy away from you? Well, I was in big trouble.

And it all started over a hill.

BACK IN THE MIDWEST we called them hills although they were reverently elevated to mountains out here in the desert. This mammoth mound of desert dirt was appropriately named Shadow Mountain, and it certainly cast a long, dark shadow over my life for many months. The firestorm had its spark in a dream.

Built at the base of Shadow Mountain, our church was carefully designed to snuggle into the rugged desert terrain. Ever conscious of the raw natural beauty, we sought to enhance and embrace our environment, providing an awe-inspiring structure for our people and the whole community.

We believe architecture is "frozen music," and we wanted to orchestrate the best for the Lord. Part of our master plan called for a simple prayer chapel to hug the steep slope of Shadow Mountain. It would provide a sanctuary of solace and spiritual refreshing for all.

The idea for a mountain prayer chapel was not new or unique. In fact, one of Arizona's most popular attractions is the magnificent Chapel of the Holy Cross in Sedona. Designed by famed architect Frank Lloyd Wright, this beautiful Catholic chapel has served as a great spiritual inspiration for people all over the world. I knew the value of such a structure and pictured a similar site for our busy and needy city.

In this small chapel I envisioned a dozen telephone prayer lines to be manned around the clock by compassionate workers caring for and helping hurting people. There would be facilities for those hikers who trudged the trails of the majestic mountain. Most important, the chapel would be a warm and loving place where all could come in privacy and pray for their unique needs, regardless of their denominational background.

Knowing we should be responsible citizens of our community, we did not make our plans clandestinely. In fact, we had discussed the chapel with Phoenix mayor Terry Goddard and received his enthusiastic approval. Then the Phoenix Mountains Preservation Council got wind of our proposal and launched an emotional campaign against the project, rejecting reason or compromise.

We became the talk of the town with a few even suggesting I was some wild cult leader with Jim Jones-like persuasion and a pocketful of money gleaned from foolish and duped attenders. Radio talk shows had a field day at our expense, and it seemed everyone wanted to go public with their comments, whether they were based on facts or not.

A flurry of newspaper articles reported that our intention was to deface the mountain and rape the environment. Editorials soon followed. They demanded that the city council condemn our property so we would be forced to sell it to the city. Then, they noted, nothing could ever be built there on the mountain. I called the newspaper editor, but he refused to present my side of the issue or even publish the architectural plans of our proposed chapel. He said flatly he would print what he wished, when he wished.

I knew we were in for trouble.

Editorial cartoonists jumped on the bandwagon with delight, portraying me in less than complimentary fashion.[1]

An editorial two days earlier had flogged our plans for a chapel. Taking liberties with both facts and issue, the editorial stated:

> Of course, the edifice the Rev. Tommy Barnett is hoping to build atop Shadow Mountain will stick out like a sore thumb. It is intended to stick out like a sore thumb.
>
> In Mr. Barnett's view, the prayer chapel he hopes to plop down in north Phoenix — on land the city ought to buy up and safely incorporate

Reprinted by permission: *The Arizona Republic*, September 18, 1988

into the Phoenix Mountains Preserve — has to be located there "to be inspirational"...

What makes Mr. Barnett's proposed structure objectionable is its intrusive nature — a 70-foot tower assaulting the sensibilities in an awesomely beautiful corner of God's wilderness.

It did not seem to matter to the editors that such a tower was never in our plans. We had considered a small spire, but the newspaper somehow concluded that we wanted to build a structure similar to the Oral Roberts prayer tower. The editorial writer went on:

Whereas others view the project as religious graffiti, Mr. Barnett sees it as outdoor advertising for the faith.[2]

Unwilling to leave the issue alone, the newspaper attacked again with another dramatic editorial a month later.

> Surely Mr. Barnett and his parishioners are among a microscopic minority who hold to the belief that a mountainside edifice of 8,000 square feet with a 70-foot-high spire thrusting heavenward is "natural" for a rugged, relatively unspoiled piece of God's handiwork. Others, alarmed at the degree to which the city's outskirts already have been defiled, think of Mr. Barnett's proposal as something close to vandalism.[3]

The editorial was accompanied by another cartoon.[4] Never-ending radio talk shows kept the controversy

Reprinted by permission: Tribune Media Services

96

going, and a biting, bylined article added to the furor. Journalist Dee J. Hall stirred up the brewing caldron by reporting:

> Some neighbors say the chapel controversy is just the latest in a series of squabbles they've had with the church at 13613 N. Cave Creek.
>
> They say dozens of buses and thousands of parishioners clog their streets each Sunday, flocking to one of Phoenix's largest churches.[5]

The reporter claimed some neighbors accused us of being insensitive to their needs, blocking their views of the mountain with our buses and "blockbusting" — that is, buying a large number of the lots and homes in an area so that the remaining residents will sell their property at bargain prices.

She concluded by insisting I had been dishonest about buying residential properties near the church and had also lied about the proposed prayer chapel.

In an effort to calm the raging storm and soothe the charged emotions, I spoke with all factions, assuring them we cared as much as they did about the stark beauty of the Arizona desert. They refused to listen — they were so entrenched in their stand against the proposal.

I was devastated.

Then support began to come in. I got a call from an old friend of mine who then worked in the White House. He told me that he knew of private funds that would help me fight all the way to the Supreme Court if necessary.

Christian television hosts called me and offered airtime to take our case to the Christian community and to set straight the lies of the media. They were also preparing to raise a "war chest" to fight for the vision God had given me.

The public and the press had gathered for a bloody shootout. The scene was to be at the "Not-So-O.K. Corral," better known as city hall. I was the target, and my opponents already had my tombstone etched.

Whenever I get in a situation like this, at first I usually feel hurt. I tend to get discouraged, and I want to say, "Just forget it." My second reaction is a desire to hold my ground and fight if I have to. In this case, I seemed to have plenty of weapons — money, Christian media, lawyers and thousands of people from my church who were ready and willing to march on city hall. After a period of time I finally get to the place where I give up my fighting and let go of my hurt. All I want then is what God wants. I have found that it's hard to find a miracle in the house until you get to this place.

When you're trying to fight the battle with your own strength, another danger arises: You are tempted to manufacture your own miracles. Remember Abraham trying to make his own miracle with his handmaiden Hagar? When Sarah couldn't give him a son, he tried to produce an heir through Hagar. The result of the union was Ishmael (Gen. 16). Later God caused Sarah to conceive, and she gave birth to Isaac (Gen. 21:2-3).

Applying that story to our situation made me realize that we could have fought and probably won — but we would have given birth to our own Ishmael. Just as the descendants of Ishmael and the descendants of Isaac were mortal enemies, we would have lived in strife from that time onward. Ishmael is a symbol of what we produce by our own efforts when we give up on our faith and patience to wait on God.

I knew further fighting would only destroy what God had brought us to Phoenix to build. This controversy would have to stop and stop quickly. Although I believed we could have fought and won this battle, we might have lost the *real* war. Our real battle and purpose were to win the lost. Anything that would divert my attention was the real enemy!

WHEN ALL THE PARTIES were gathered together at city hall on the appointed day, I stood and asked for the floor. Before the first shot could be fired, I publicly apologized, saying, "I want you all to know that we had no intention to be anything but a blessing to the city. Whether we build on the side of the mountain has no bearing. We're going to keep doing what we are doing — feeding the hungry, clothing the naked...."

The shootout fizzled when I refused to fight, and those whom I felt were "the bad guys" had to holster their loaded verbal weapons. The city council quickly agreed to the demands of the Phoenix Mountains Preservation Council, who had wanted our land all along. We later learned they had resented our buying the property because they fully expected the previous owner to give it to them. When he failed to make the gift, they took their wrath out on us.

Some city council members tried to mollify us by praising our church for its work with children, the elderly, the homeless and the handicapped. Councilman Howard Adams even told the press, "It's nice to hear the pastor plans to continue his good works, just a little closer to sea level."[6] Assistant parks director L. B. Scacewater admitted, "I think it was just so emotional [that] it got out of hand."[7]

Things certainly had gotten out of hand, and it was no fun being caught in the vortex of public disapproval. Although this was not an altogether new position for me, it still stung and threw me off balance for some time. It was only on my knees that I found perspective and learned to rise above the squabble so I could keep my eyes on the real battle — the battle for the lost souls of dying men and women.

I had wanted to fight to the finish in order to claim our miracle. I had my faith in full gear for the prayer chapel. I hate accepting defeat, but something inside me was saying, Give it up, Tommy.

IT SEEMED AT THAT time there was no miracle to be found in this situation. The only good to come out of it was perhaps the humbling of Tommy Barnett. But as I said earlier, the miracle that God wants to give you often comes in the most unexpected ways.

The first miracle that happened as a result of this altercation with the press and city officials was related to the sale of our property to the city council. This piece of land was on a very steep part of the mountain. It was really only valuable to us because we wanted to build on it. In addition, the cost of building on the property would have been high. However, because of all the furor the commission stirred up about it, the value of those eleven acres skyrocketed. We finally sold them for $1.2 million, four times the previous value. That was half of what we originally paid for the entire seventy acres of property!

There was another financial miracle that happened as a direct result of this controversy. One of our deacons had a retired friend named Scott Shady. Scott knew about the church and how many things were being done to help hurting and needy people from every segment of society in Phoenix. He was so upset about how the newspaper had misrepresented us that he decided to give the church a large sum of money, and he became a more dedicated Christian.

A third miracle that came out of this was favor with the media.

This miracle started with Mayor Terry Goddard, who was not pleased with what had happened. Before allowing the city hall meeting to adjourn, he took a swipe at those who opposed our plan. He criticized the park staff for not informing him that our land was considered to be a high-priority parcel for the preserve. He told the council and press of his meeting with me years before and how he had heartily endorsed the chapel plan because he was operating under the assumption the city did not want or need the land. The mayor felt the matter had not been handled properly and wanted the press, public and council to know his position.

I was invited to many radio talk shows. We were exonerated, the dirty tricks of the commission were exposed, and we have enjoyed great favor with the media ever since.

DON'T LET TROUBLES KEEP you from the making of a miracle! That doesn't necessarily mean you should forge ahead, bulldozing everything in your path. If we had done that, we would have missed God's miracle for us.

You will get offtrack if you think you know for sure exactly what kind of miracle God wants to give you. Remember that miracles come from surprising places in unexpected ways. You have to trust that God is working all things together for good according to His great plan. Do everything you can to flow with His plan rather than trying to force Him to bless yours.

GOD LOVES YOU AND has a wonderful plan for your life!" That's law number one in Campus Crusade's *Four Spiritual Laws* tract. Part of that wonderful plan is to bring us to Christian maturity and to perfect our faith — but sometimes that process doesn't seem so wonderful.

The apostle Peter said we were "protected by the power of God through faith" (1 Pet. 1:5). You would think that protection would include the attacks of deceptive and antagonistic newspaper reporters. I've found that God watches over us more than we will ever know. But I've also discovered that His purposes are sometimes worked out through circumstances that we would rather avoid.

After saying we are protected by God, Peter continues with these words:

> IN this you greatly rejoice, even though now for a little while, if necessary, you have been distressed by various trials
> [7]that the proof of your faith, being more precious than gold which is perishable, even though tested by fire, may be found to result in praise

and glory and honor at the revelation of Jesus
Christ.

1 Peter 1:6-7

In the final analysis we had won a great victory in the
Phoenix prayer chapel controversy. One of the benefits of
that agonizing experience was the proving and maturing
of our faith. Perhaps, in God's eyes, that was the most
valuable part of all, for He knew that our troubles with
the media were not over.

Officials of my denomination called and asked that I
cooperate with an article being written by the *Wall Street
Journal* about the Assemblies of God. They assured me
this was to be a good piece which would help the denomination recover from the bad press after the disaster of the
television scandals. They had been approached by the
prestigious paper and promised that a major positive fea-
ture would bring into balance all the negative and unfair
publicity the movement had been receiving. I hesitated
because I knew firsthand what a prejudiced press could
do. However, the officials persisted, so I reluctantly
agreed to cooperate.

Reporter Robert Johnson soon showed up assuring me
of his good intentions underlining all that my denominational leaders had said. He was all smiles, and I was
immediately drawn to this "open-minded" man.

Setting aside many hours from my demanding schedule, I took the journalist for tours through our facilities
and among our various outreaches in the city. He seemed
genuinely impressed and often commented on what a
wonderful work we were doing. The culmination of our
time came when he attended our Sunday morning service
and came to the altar in response to my call for conversion. When he left, he assured us we would be most
pleased with the positive article the *Journal* would do.

I relaxed too soon, and it did not take me long to realize
I, and many others, had been duped.

Featured on the front page of the *Wall Street Journal*, under the headline "Heavenly Gifts," were several subheads setting the tone of the slashing story. These journalistic hooks shouted, "Preaching a Gospel of Acquisitiveness, a Showy Sect Prospers" and "After TV-Minister Scandals, Assemblies of God Emerge Bigger, Richer Than Ever." The last pejorative subhead proclaimed, "Praying for a Honda Accord." Then the real attack started.

Ignoring other pastors and Assemblies of God officials, the story started with a cynical slam of me. The reporter then attacked the denomination, citing inaccurate statistics and suggesting that our worship style is more fluff than substance. An Assemblies of God spokesperson was misquoted as saying, "The image of a cosmic Santa Claus has crept into our church."

The *Wall Street Journal* article smelled more like a tabloid attack than a balanced report of a responsible newspaper. Nothing was said about all the good work our people do in touching the hurting and helpless of our city.

When the *Wall Street Journal* article came out, the calls and letters started to come in. Some suggested I sue the *Journal*. Others were angry because all our hard work among the homeless, hurting and helpless was totally ignored by the article. Every day I had calls, letters and faxes telling me what I should do in response.

The general superintendent of the Assemblies of God, G. Raymond Carlson, wrote, "I have tried to call you several times in recent days since the job the reporter did on us in the *Wall Street Journal*. He made every approach as being on the level, but in turn did a piece of dishonest journalism. Possibly Matthew 5:11-12 would be helpful at this point."

The Scripture passage that superintendent Carlson called to my attention simply says:

BLESSED are you when men cast insults at you, and persecute you, and say all kinds of evil against you falsely, on account of Me.

[12]Rejoice, and be glad, for your reward in heaven is great, for so they persecuted the prophets who were before you.

Matthew 5:11-12

Finally, I did do something. I wrote a letter to Robert Johnson. Here is what it said:

Dear Rob:

Choice Christian greetings!

Although your article has brought me much distress, my real heartbreak is that I apparently failed to be a good witness of Jesus Christ to you.

Rob, if my words and actions in any way offended you or were a bad example, I ask you to please forgive me. I have examined my heart before God in prayer and have asked Him to remove anything from my life that should not be there.

I really did enjoy my time with you and found you to be a very likable, nice man. I do truly love you, Rob, and if at any time I can be a blessing in any way, please just contact me.

Again, please forgive me! In our short day together I felt you are earnestly seeking for God and reality. And, although we might have turned you off by our methods, please keep your eyes on Him Who never fails! I pray for you every day and I would appreciate it if you would also pray for me.

Your friend,
Tommy Barnett

P.S. A reply is not necessary.

There is a simple and spiritual reason I wrote that letter and meant every word of it. I had to. I had to forgive because you can't move forward looking in the rearview mirror!

My church did not need a bitter pastor. They deserved better. The hurt I experienced was so small compared to the gaping wounds of our world. If I spend all my time licking my own wounds, I cannot help heal the wounds of others. Therefore, I had to make a conscious and determined decision to let go of my hurts and anger so I could get on with my reason for being. It was not important for the *Journal* reporter to apologize, ask forgiveness or even acknowledge my letter. But it was important that I take my eyes off the rearview mirror and lift them to the whitened harvest all around me.

As I pondered how to respond to the unfairness dealt me, I was taken back to the cross and the example of our Lord in His last moments. There is a stirring and startling scene that grabs me and holds me in check when I am tempted to react too quickly. The Scripture says, "And when they had come to a place called Golgotha, which means Place of a Skull, they gave him wine to drink mingled with gall; and after tasting it, he was unwilling to drink it" (Matt. 27:33-34).

Christ tasted the gall, but He spit it out!

Gall was a poisonous herb growing spontaneously in the furrows of the fields in Israel. Frequently this wild weed, or gourd, was mixed with wine to make a stupefying drink powerful enough to shut off pain for a season. Gall was brutally bitter, and during Jeremiah's day sore punishment was likened to a drink of gall water. We are not told whether Jesus was offered the drink out of mercy or meanness. All we know is that when He tasted the wine mixed with gall, He spit it out.

Life is so structured that at times we will be handed wine mixed with gall. If we are to be like Jesus, we must spit out the bitterness, refusing to ingest it.

It is always tempting to drink wine mixed with gall when we are being "crucified." When we hurt so badly, anything that makes the pain stop for even a moment feels good. Self-pity and bitterness are like gall. It will ease pain momentarily as we justify our position and slash out at those who are hurting us. But bitterness will also kill us! The Bible warns, "Watch out that no bitterness takes root among you, for as it springs up it causes deep trouble, hurting many in their spiritual lives" (Heb. 12:14-15, TLB).

Tragically, many are like the lady living in the early part of this century who was bitten by a rabid dog. She immediately got a pad and pencil and started writing down a long list of names. When asked why she was doing this, she replied, "These are the people I plan to bite before I die."

Raymond Carlson gave the right advice: Rejoice and be glad when you are persecuted and lied about for His name's sake. But you can't rejoice unless you spit out the gall of bitterness.

The present pain will pass, but how we react and respond during these tense and testing times will follow forever. After I had written that letter to Rob Johnson, my spirits soared. I was free again!

There was a new spring to my step and a new note in my song. I enjoyed preaching, and my heart overflowed with love for the wonderful people God had given me. I saw sunshine everywhere I looked. I forgave and forgot for my own sake — and in doing so found fullness of life!

Making Trouble Become Your Servant

I want to give you one principle that has changed my life and our church. Speaking through the prophet Jeremiah, God made this comment:

NEBUCHADNEZZAR king of Babylon, My servant....

Jeremiah 25:9

I can understand why Abraham, Moses, Job, Joshua

106

and others were called "My servant." But Nebuchadnez-zar? This wicked, ruthless, vile and merciless king?

Nebuchadnezzar hated everything about God. He hated the house of God. He destroyed Jerusalem, the temple and the altar and carried the vessels used in worship to Babylon. He hated the people of God. Most were killed, and many were taken into captivity and treated as slaves.

It is as if God were saying, "This wicked king hates Me and is trying to destroy My work, My people and My house. He would try to destroy Me if he could. He thinks he's trying to hurt My people, but I'll make him My servant instead. I'll confound his plans and use his evil intentions for good."

We can also cause our adversaries and our troubles to become our servants.

What you are, you have made yourself. By yielding to Satan and his pressures, you can allow adversities to break your spirit and destroy you. Your troubles can become a stumbling block, or they can become a stepping stone that lifts you to higher ground. They can become your master, or they can become your servant.

I have determined that I will use my adversity and opposition as my servants, and you can do the same thing.

Remember when the newspaper editor refused to hear my side of the story and declared that he could print anything he wanted? *The Arizona Republic* and *The Phoenix Gazette* determined to be my opponents, but God caused their unjustified criticism to be a servant to Phoenix First Assembly and to me.

There are people who experience what seems to be much more than their share of difficulties. The hard times make some bitter and others better. Some have allowed past problems to spoil their faith. Whenever they face a new challenge, all they can think of are the problems of the past. They sound like broken records reciting them. Consequently, they have little faith that anything will ever turn out good for them.

Gideon was like that. The Midianites had invaded and brutally dominated the children of Israel. Like many people today, Gideon had difficulty believing the God of miracles was with them because of all the troubles they had encountered.

THEN the angel of the Lord came and sat under the oak that was in Ophrah, which belonged to Joash the Abiezrite as his son Gideon was beating out wheat in the wine press in order to save it from the Midianites.

¹²And the angel of the Lord appeared to him and said to him, "The Lord is with you, O valiant warrior."

¹³Then Gideon said to him, "O my lord, if the Lord is with us, why then has all this happened to us? And where are all His miracles which our fathers told us about, saying, 'Did not the Lord bring us up from Egypt?' But now the Lord has abandoned us and given us into the hand of Midian."

¹⁴And the Lord looked at him and said, "Go in this your strength and deliver Israel from the hand of Midian. Have I not sent you?"

Judges 6:11-14

The occupation of the Midianites had its purpose in the discipline of the children of Israel. But it was also an opportunity for Gideon. If he was to be used by God in a historic dimension, Gideon would first have to forget what was behind and move ahead in faith. He had to quit nursing the problems of the past.

Troubles can be your servant, or they can keep you from the making of a miracle. They can be your stepping stone or your stumbling block. They can make you better or just bitter.

It's up to you.

NINE

Pass on to
the Positive

WHEN THE church initially got into the conflict with the media and city officials over the prayer chapel, I felt some real anxiety. Only those very close to me knew how troubled I was.

One of the ten commandments for the making of a miracle is this: Don't be blinded by negativism, but pass on to the positive (see chapter 2).

When a crisis like this takes place, the first inclination is to worry. It sometimes takes me a couple of days to get back into a positive frame of mind. But after I get over those first few days, people ask how I can be so joyful in the midst of such a mess.

I always try to keep a good attitude. Certainly I have my moments when I'm not on top of things, but I'm always working on my frame of mind. If I didn't work on it so much, I wouldn't do as well as I do. We all need to know better how to fight the battle against negativism and pass on to the positive.

Creating a Monster in Your House

You never come to be something or someone you did not first become in your thoughts. The wise man said, "As he thinketh in his heart, so is he" (Prov. 23:7, KJV). Who you are is a direct result of what you think.

Jesus instructed us not to be worried or anxious about our lives, our clothing or our food. We shouldn't waste time on worry because the things we worry about so rarely come to pass anyway.

Worry and anxiety won't do anything to help fix a real problem, either. That was Jesus' point when He asked, "Which of you by being anxious can add a single cubit to his life's span?" (Luke 12:25). His rhetorical question implies that no one can.

Worrying about Goliath's threats did nothing to help the Israelite army defeat him (1 Sam. 17). Worrying won't make your problems go away either. But there is one thing that meditating on and mulling over your predicament will do for you. It will create a monster inside you.

Like most monsters, this one is small when he is born, but he has a voracious appetite. Every time you entertain negative, fearful thoughts about the problem at hand, you feed the little monster. And, of course, he grows. He really loves those negative thoughts. Imagining the worst possible way a situation could end up is the sweetest treat of all for him.

He's never satisfied and always wants more. If you feed

him enough, the thought monster inside you will become bigger, hungrier and more difficult to kill. In fact, he will grow to be even bigger than the external problem that spawned him. He can also be more dangerous. The fear of losing your job can take on a more destructive aspect in your life than the actual consequences of being laid off.

Some people grow very fond of their monster and love to feed him. They don't really want their problems to go away. Then they'd have no negative thoughts with which to feed their pet. But if their problems do go away, they will quickly find more to take their place.

Are you feeding any pet monsters in your life? They are fun to play with for a little while, but be careful. They'll eat your dreams, your hopes and your faith. They'll destroy your life.

THE ONLY WAY TO get rid of these guys is to starve them. Paul gave the prescription for victory over anxiety and negativism.

> BE anxious for nothing, but in everything by prayer and supplication with thanksgiving let your requests be made known to God.
>
> ⁷And the peace of God, which surpasses all comprehension, shall guard your hearts and your minds in Christ Jesus.
>
> ⁸Finally, brethren, whatever is true, whatever is honorable, whatever is right, whatever is pure, whatever is lovely, whatever is of good repute, if there is any excellence and if anything worthy of praise, let your mind dwell on these things.
>
> ⁹The things you have learned and received and heard and seen in me, practice these things; and the God of peace shall be with you.
>
> Philippians 4:6-9

One of the ways to stop feeding the monster is to think about something else. You may believe you are helping somebody by sitting with them hour after hour, day after day, talking about their problems. But, in effect, you are indirectly helping them feed their anxiety.

The most important thing both of you can do is get your minds back on God. If you release your problem to God and stop worrying about it, it becomes God's problem. But when you start worrying, it becomes your problem again.

Problems are perpetuated in direct proportion to the amount of thought you give them. You will discover that the problem loses its power over you as you stop meditating on it.

> YOU will keep him in perfect peace,
> Whose mind is stayed on You.
>
> Isaiah 26:3, NKJV

The Secret Chamber

Ezekiel was sitting in his house one day with the elders of Judah when "the hand of the Lord God fell" on him (Ezek. 8:1). He saw a brightly glowing heavenly figure that "stretched out the form of a hand," picked him up by the hair of his head and transported him in a vision to the temple in Jerusalem (Ezek. 8:3).

At the north gate of the inner court, Ezekiel saw people worshipping an idol that was called the "image of Lust" (Ezek. 8:5, NEB). The heavenly being said to him:

> SON of man, do you see what they are doing, the great abominations which the house of Israel are committing here, that I should be far from My sanctuary? But yet you will see still greater abominations.
>
> Ezekiel 8:6

As bad as the offense was in the court of the temple, there was still something more sinister taking place out of sight. Elijah was taken to a place near the entrance to the inner court and was shown a hole in the wall. Ezekiel was instructed to dig through the place in the wall, and, having done so, he found an entranceway and a passage that led to a secret chamber.

> AND He [the heavenly being] said to me, "Go in and see the wicked abominations that they are committing here."
> ¹⁰So I entered and looked, and behold, every form of creeping things and beasts and detestable things, with all the idols of the house of Israel, were carved on the wall all around.
> ¹¹And standing in front of them were seventy elders of the house of Israel, with Jaazaniah the son of Shaphan standing among them, each man with his censer in his hand, and the fragrance of the cloud of incense rising.
> ¹²Then He said to me, "Son of man, do you see what the elders of the house of Israel are committing in the dark, each man in the room of his carved images? For they say, 'The Lord does not see us; the Lord has forsaken the land.'"
> Ezekiel 8:9-12

The elders of Israel were having secret meetings in a hidden chamber where they burned incense to their images and idols. This was taking place in the temple, not far from the most holy place and from the court where the sacrifices were offered on the altar.

Ezekiel's vision provides a good illustration for us and challenges us to consider what is going on in our temple.

The New Testament teaches that we as Christians are the temple of God because the Holy Spirit lives in us. Think of the burning of incense as a person's meditations and thought life.

Among those things offered up as sacrifices in our temple are our thoughts. We are to offer up "a sacrifice of praise, the fruit of lips that give thanks to His name" (Heb. 13:15). David said, "Let the words of my mouth and the meditation of my heart be acceptable in Thy sight, O Lord, my rock and my Redeemer" (Ps. 19:14).

Every person has a secret chamber in his heart. No one sees what it contains or what goes on in there. No one but the Lord, that is.

Are there dark, secret chambers in your temple where incense is burning to images it shouldn't be? Are there images or altars of lust, hatred and jealousy? If so, you need to cleanse the dark closets because God sees even in the darkest and most hidden of places.

There is another sin of the mind that is represented here. The Scripture says that the elders were burning incense in the dark, "each man in the room of his carved images," because, they said, "the Lord does not see us; the Lord has forsaken the land" (Ezek. 8:12).

Apparently a series of trials and tribulations had caused them to give up on their faith in God. They assumed that He had forsaken them.

Going through difficult times will either make you bitter or better. Unfortunately, the pain, discouragement and disappointment of the past have gotten the best of some. In the secret chambers of their thoughts they continually burn incense to images of resentment, fear and the pain of disappointment.

It's time for us to pull down the idols, rid ourselves of the images and get back to offering the acceptable sacrifices of praise and worship. The apostle Paul said we should be "casting down imaginations, and every high thing that exalteth itself against the knowledge of God, and bringing into captivity every thought to the obedience of Christ" (2 Cor. 10:5, KJV).

SOMETIMES YOU HAVE TO think things through to come up with answers. You don't have to deny that difficulties exist, but *how* you think about them is what will make the difference. You should look at the problems in the light of this fact: For the unlimited God you serve, all things are possible.

God can solve a problem in a thousand ways. When you look at the obstacles in that frame of mind, He will reveal one of those solutions. My advice is that you don't consider your problems until you have the faith to see them from God's perspective. Try imagining ten different ways God could work things out for you.

You need to take your thoughts captive before they take you captive. Remember: whatever you are or will be started with your thoughts. Don't grow a thought monster inside that you will have to feed forever. Don't burn incense on the altar of resentment, doubt and fear. Don't be blinded by negativism.

Pass on to the positive.

TEN

The More You're Spilled, the More You're Filled

AS PASTOR of Phoenix First Assembly of God, I spend much of my time trying to provide ways for people to pour; that is, ways for people to use what they have.

That's why we have 180 outreach ministries. Even if they did nothing for the people we are trying to reach, pouring out is essential for our own sakes. We are only happy and we only grow when we are pouring into empty vessels.

When you dam up streams of water, they become stagnant. Fish die in stagnant water. In that way, many churches have become dead seas rather than flowing rivers.

I have often heard people talking about how "Spirit-filled" a church or a person was. In our consumer-driven society I think we have twisted the meaning and purpose of being Spirit-filled.

Sometimes we describe Christian experiences like merit badges.

"Are you born again?"

"Have you been water baptized?"

"Are you filled with the Holy Spirit?"

These are not awards to be displayed like patches on your sleeve. They are parts of a dynamic and ongoing relationship with God.

"Oh, yes, I was filled with the Spirit back in 1972," I've heard people say. Sometimes I want to ask if it had occurred to them that they might have leaked a little since then.

Peter and John were dragged before the counsel of the scribes and Pharisees (the Sanhedrin) to give an account of how they had healed the lame man who sat outside the gate of the temple.

> AND when they had placed them in the center, they began to inquire, "By what power, or in what name, have you done this?"
> [8]Then Peter, filled with the Holy Spirit, said to them....
>
> Acts 4:7-8

The literal rendering of the text is noted in the margin of many translations. In the New American Standard it reads: "having just been filled with the Holy Spirit." Peter was filled with the Holy Spirit, and then he spoke out in boldness.

The same phrase is used again referring to Paul in Cyprus when he confronted Elymas the magician.

BUT Saul, who was also known as Paul, [having just been] filled with the Holy Spirit, fixed his gaze upon him.

Acts 13:9

The text goes on to say that Paul proclaimed that Elymas would be blinded because of his opposition to the gospel. It happened as Paul declared, and as a result the proconsul believed.

When Peter and John returned from their confrontation with the scribes and Pharisees over the healing of the lame man, they reported to the rest the threats that had been issued; that is, that they should not preach anymore in the name of Jesus. All that were present lifted up their voices in prayer. As a result the place where they gathered was shaken, and they were "all filled with the Holy Spirit, and began to speak the word of God with boldness" (Acts 4:31).

Here were all these apostles and disciples being filled with the Holy Spirit again!

Some Pentecostals and evangelicals have differing ideas about the baptism of the Spirit as a second blessing. But regardless of your belief about theology and terminology, we all need to be filled with the Holy Spirit, continually, regularly, daily.

I pray for power every morning — even beg for God's power. I believe God likes to hear me dependent on Him! I have little signs I post in my car and office that read: "Pray for power." I had these little notes printed up for our church, too. Our people have them stuck up everywhere.

Paul exhorted the Ephesians to be filled with the Spirit (Eph. 5:18). The use of the present tense form of the Greek verb *plerousthe*, "be filled," signifies that being filled with the Spirit is a continuous and repetitive process.[1]

For the apostles, being filled with the Holy Spirit was not something that happened only once. It was an ongoing occurrence that always resulted in a demonstration of love and service to others.

No one has any need to be filled unless he or she intends to be poured. And the more you are poured, the more you are refilled.

The more appropriate question would be: Are you Spirit-spilled?

Getting blessed, being touched or even "falling under the power" is not the same as being Spirit-filled. The measure of our spirituality should be not how much we get but how much we give — how much of the Spirit and grace of God flows through us, not just to us.

I have heard people talk about how much they love a particular church because they really get blessed there. You need to get blessed in church, but it is more important that you become a blessing and become someone else's miracle.

People argue about the biblical pattern of being filled with the Spirit and the corresponding theological implications. If the biblical pattern tells us anything, it is that being filled with God's Spirit turns you into a lover and a giver (1 John 4:12-13).

EVERY YEAR AT CHRISTMASTIME I ask our people to go out and buy a present for a hurting, underprivileged child in our city. They can spend as much as they want, but it has to be worth five dollars or more. I also ask them to pray that God will lead them to the present He wants them to buy.

They bring their presents in and put them at the foot of our huge singing Christmas tree. Last year we brought in about eight thousand underprivileged kids to our church for a special Christmas program. At the end of the service, we led all the children into the auditorium.

The orchestra and the two hundred people standing on the forty-five-foot singing Christmas tree led the congregation in singing carols as the children came in to find two mountains of presents under the tree, one for the boys and one for the girls.

Every year when those children come down the aisle, the adults in our congregation weep and cry so much they can hardly sing.

Dear reader, please hear this: If it didn't bless any of those kids, I would continue to give away presents for the sake of our congregation. Every person who puts a present under that tree has the opportunity to pour into an empty vessel. They have found that the joy of the Lord comes from pouring.

One of the little boys asked his bus pastor to pray with him that he would get an electric train for Christmas.

"Do you think God would give me an electric train?" he asked.

The bus pastor really didn't know what to say as they prayed together. He was afraid that a disappointment could destroy the little boy's faith. He knew that someone in the church might buy a train. But the presents were wrapped and given out randomly. Nobody knew who would get what package. But, as you can guess, someone in the church was led to buy a Lionel electric train set. And, out of all the other presents, that's the one the little boy received.

That young man will never forget that, in the midst of eight thousand dirty, rambunctious little kids, he was so special to God that his prayer was heard and answered. But it was no less of a blessing for that family who had the privilege of seeing a miracle happen as they poured into an empty vessel.

The Kingdom Invisible Appears

Temperatures well over 100 degrees in Phoenix are not as uncomfortable as 90-degree weather in other places. The reason is the low humidity in Arizona. There is very little moisture in the air.

Even in areas with low humidity, however, there is always some water in the air all around us. We breathe it, and sometimes we can feel it on a muggy day.

The dew point is the temperature at which that moisture in the air begins to form into water droplets. When that happens at high altitudes, the droplets fall as rain. The coolness of the evening causes dew drops to form on the ground.

It is at the dew point that the invisible reality of airborne water becomes visible.

God is like the moisture in the air: He's everywhere. Theologians use the word *omnipresent*, which means present at all places at the same time. The power, glory and love of God are all around us, but His kingdom is invisible to our eyes.

When the nature and character of God are displayed through His servants, the kingdom becomes a little more visible. When miracles occur, we begin to realize how close God really is. This was true with the feeding of the five thousand, the water turned to wine at Cana, the great catch of fish from the other side of the boat and so on.

When we give in faith and pour into others, the invisible kingdom of God manifests itself. When the widow began to pour into the empty vessels, the kingdom invisible became the kingdom visible.

One of the kids at the Christmas party looked up and saw that huge singing Christmas tree, the lights, the presents. He turned to his bus pastor and said, "Is this heaven?"

In a way, yes, it was, not the place we go to spend eternal life, but a visible manifestation of the kingdom of God.

What made it happen? People gave.

It seemed like heaven for the little boy, but it seemed that way even more so for the members of our church, because by pouring into those empty vessels they felt the nearness of the presence of God.

The Giving-ness of God

God gives life and breath to all mankind, He gives grace and mercy irrespective of our unworthiness, and He gave His only Son for us because He so loved the world. God is a giver! There is a beautiful song that goes: "Out of His infinite mercy in Jesus, He giveth and giveth and giveth again."[2]

When you look at the giving-ness of God, you peer right into His very heart and nature. It is the very essence of who He is. We are not offered forgiveness because we deserve it, nor do we live and breathe because we are worthy of it or go to heaven because we have earned it. God is love, and love gives freely.

There are two ways you can live: either as a giver, who is becoming more and more like God, or as a taker, preoccupied with self. The Bible says that no man can see God and live (Ex. 33:20). When you see the giving-ness in the heart of God, you will begin to die to your selfishness, your grasping and your acquisitive nature. That, however, is when you really begin to live.

The Pouring Principle

A man cried out of the crowd, asking Jesus to settle an issue between his brother and him. Apparently, one of the brothers was hoarding the family inheritance.

AND He said to them, "Beware, and be on your guard against every form of greed; for not even when one has an abundance does his life consist of his possessions."
[16]And He told them a parable, saying, "The land of a certain rich man was very productive.

¹⁷"And he began reasoning to himself, saying, 'What shall I do, since I have no place to store my crops?'

¹⁸"And he said, 'This is what I will do: I will tear down my barns and build larger ones, and there I will store all my grain and my goods.

¹⁹" 'And I will say to my soul, "Soul, you have many goods laid up for many years to come; take your ease, eat, drink and be merry." '

²⁰"But God said to him, 'You fool! This very night your soul is required of you; and now who will own what you have prepared?'

²¹"So is the man who lays up treasure for himself, and is not rich toward God."

Luke 12:15-21

The rich man was not a fool because he was rich. God loves prosperous and successful people. But it had never occurred to this rich man that his prosperity was a gift from God for the purpose of pouring abundantly into others. One man in our church, whose business has been very productive, buys 250 brand-new bicycles each year at Christmas for the needy kids. But this rich man Jesus spoke of hoarded it all for himself.

One of the greatest hindrances to real joy is that we let our perceptions and behavior be determined by those who want to sell us something. American commercials tell us constantly that value, self-worth and happiness come from what we can obtain. In other words, our lives consist of our possessions.

Wrong!

Our culture and the media driving it teach us what is contrary to the kingdom of God — that joy comes from abundant possessions rather than abundant giving.

This even finds its way into our churches. We are instructed to give so that we can get more. The operant words there are *so that*. The misguided force behind this teaching is that life comes from abundant possessiveness.

To be a cheerful giver means that I'm not giving to get more, all along thinking that life is in the return. A cheerful giver pours because he believes that life is in the pouring.

Those who feign cheerfulness but in reality only rejoice in the thought of their "hundred-fold return" will eventually hoard their blessings.

That kind of giving is like playing the stock market. You invest to get a greater return, to reinvest for even greater returns and so on until you take the cash and run. The point all along was to hoard.

THE MIRACLE OF MULTIPLICATION continued as long as the widow continued to pour. The miracle of abundant life continues in our hearts as long as we continue to be "Spirit-spilled." If you stop giving, you will certainly dry up as a Christian, and your vessel will be empty. Always keep yourself in a position in which you are able to give.

The widow at Zarephath must have surely hesitated to give her last meal to Elijah. But having given it in faith, there was a miracle in her house. The oil and flour were not exhausted (1 Kin. 17:16).

Taking the time, effort and expense to pour into empty vessels is not a drain. Rather it is invigorating. I always receive back more than I give. That's why after so many years I'm not feeling burned out.

So what are you looking for? Are you looking for what you can get out of life, or are you looking for what you can pour out in life? Are you going to be a giver or a taker? Make a decision right now: I am going to pour into empty vessels and be a Spirit-spilled Christian.

ELEVEN

The Miracle's in the Bush

ONCE AGAIN exhaustion overcame me. I pulled over to the side of the road and stopped the car. It was only seventeen miles from my church to my home, but I had to stop and sleep until I regained the strength to continue.

I had been feeling this way for about three or four months, and I was at my wit's end. I had always jogged five to seven miles a day and played basketball in the church basketball league. I was an extremely active person physically. Even my family noticed the difference. When we vacationed in Hawaii, I spent most of the two weeks in my hotel room. I would get up in the morning and be so tired that I didn't even want to go to the beach. We knew something was wrong.

I was puzzled, but I knew I was God's property and decided to leave it in His hands. If He wanted me to stay in the ministry, He would give me the strength to do it.

Finally I could hide it no longer. Because of the church building program, I was forced to go to the doctor. The bank had asked me to insure the loan; I had to take out a life insurance policy for $7 million to cover the cost of the church. If something happened to me and I couldn't guarantee the loan, the bank would get their money. For that kind of life insurance policy I needed to see several doctors.

I visited the first doctor and took the required test. The report came back, stating that I had a very serious heart condition and was not insurable. I went to two more doctors who gave the same report. We were planning to pursue treatment the following week.

I told George Zimmer, our business manager, what the doctors had said. "Don't tell the church," I cautioned him. "The church doesn't need a sick pastor."

Of all things that Sunday, after my visit to the doctors, I preached on healing.

After the service George came up to me and said, "Tommy, I believe God will heal you if you believe."

"Let's pray," I said.

George laid hands on me and prayed.

Two or three days later he came to me and said, "You look better."

I feel better, I thought.

"Have you been tired?" he asked me.

"No," I told him.

"I believe God healed you," he said.

"How about that?" I said. "I think He did."

We decided I should verify my healing with more medical tests. George said he was going to call Dr. Edward Diethrich to schedule an appointment for me. Dr. Diethrich is a world-renowned heart doctor. In fact, one of our board members, Allan Mayer, the owner of the Oscar Mayer company, was on Dr. Diethrich's board. He personally asked the doctor to test my heart.

At the doctor's office, we went through two days of extensive testing. At the end of those tests, he said to me, "You're the picture of health. There is nothing wrong with your heart. Your heart is great."

God healed me. Now I go every year for checkups for my insurance. After eight years they have never found anything wrong with my heart.

ALL THE BLESSINGS ABRAHAM had received meant nothing unless he had an heir to whom he could pass them on. Isaac was the miracle child, the miracle in Abraham's house. And it was through this miracle that all the promises of God to Abraham were going to be realized. Abraham had been promised that his descendants would be as numerous as the dust of the earth and the stars of the heavens (Gen. 13:16; 15:5).

Old Abe might not have been sure he would live to see those descendants, but in Isaac he saw them all. Without Isaac none of the promises of God to him would ever come to pass. Isaac was to Abraham and his promise what my voice was to me and my promise.

NOW it came about after these things, that God tested Abraham, and said to him, "Abraham!" And he said, "Here I am."
²And He said, "Take now your son, your only son, whom you love, Isaac, and go to the land of Moriah; and offer him there as a burnt offering on one of the mountains of which I will tell you."

Genesis 22:1-2

You've got to learn to hold the promises of God lightly. Jesus didn't grasp at His rightful position (Phil. 2:6-7). He laid it aside and as a result was exalted by the Father to be the King of kings and Lord of lords.

If God has truly given you a promise, a vision, a gift or a ministry, you don't have to grasp for it. It is in His hands to bring it to pass. If you hold it too tightly, the gift can eventually become more precious to you than God who gave it.

Though it surely made no sense to Abraham, he set about to do what God had commanded. He ascended the mountain, built the altar and bound his son.

AND Abraham stretched out his hand, and took the knife to slay his son.

11But the angel of the Lord called to him from heaven, and said, "Abraham, Abraham!" And he said, "Here I am."

12And he said, "Do not stretch out your hand against the lad, and do nothing to him; for now I know that you fear God, since you have not withheld your son, your only son, from Me."

13Then Abraham raised his eyes and looked, and behold, behind him a ram caught in the thicket by his horns; and Abraham went and took the ram, and offered him up for a burnt offering in the place of his son.

Genesis 22:10-13

To Abraham, following this God who first spoke to him in Ur certainly had a lot of emotional ups and downs. He left civilization to become a wanderer in the wilderness. He waited for his promised child to be born to his ninety-year-old wife. Now this. But he learned to walk the walk of faith, and it was because of this faith that he received the promises.

It is worth noting that Abraham didn't recognize that the

ram was stuck in the bush until he had passed God's test. In the same way, you will often be unable to see that your miracle is also in the bush until you pass the test by putting your desire and your vision on the altar — even if those visions and desires are something you think God has given you.

Sometimes the key to finding your miracle is letting go and letting God fulfill His promise.

When God called me to go to Davenport, I thought, Surely this offer is just a test. But sometimes it's no test. God actually wanted something put on the altar. In that case, it was my desire for a big church. But if I had persisted in grasping my vision and what I thought was God's means of fulfilling His promise to me, I would have missed the greatest blessing of all.

Worshipping the Source of Your Miracle

Putting your gifts, abilities and even the promises God gives you on the altar is an act of worship to God. If you refuse to do so, it is because you have begun to worship the gift, the talent or the vision God has given you.

It would be like the widow worshipping the bottle from which the oil continued to pour. When God moves on our behalf, we tend to try to pass on to the next generation the instrument or the method God uses to send us our miracle. Eventually we will make relics out of the instruments of God's blessings.

People have always had the tendency to forget that the source of their miracle is God.

Bronze Serpents Last a Long Time

When the children of Israel were being led through the wilderness, they often complained and rebelled against the Lord and against Moses. On one occasion the Lord sent fiery serpents among the people. Many were bitten and died.

They came to Moses repenting of their sin and asking him to intercede for them that God would remove the serpents.

> THEN the Lord said to Moses, "Make a fiery serpent, and set it on a standard; and it shall come about, that everyone who is bitten, when he looks at it, he shall live."
>
> 9And Moses made a bronze serpent and set it on the standard; and it came about, that if a serpent bit any man, when he looked to the bronze serpent, he lived.
>
> Numbers 21:8-9

It wasn't the serpent that healed the people; it was God. Yet who could ever forget the significance of that bronze serpent?

Of course, God told Moses to make the serpent, but Moses was the one who decided to make it out of bronze. He might have done better to have made the serpent out of something more perishable. Bronze serpents tend to last a very long time.

More than five hundred years later in the midst of the spiritually dark ages of Israel there arose a young king named Hezekiah. Though his father, King Ahaz, was thoroughly wicked, Hezekiah led a revival that brought Israel back from apostasy. The first order of revival business in those days was the destruction of the altars used for pagan idol worship.

> AND he [Hezekiah] did right in the sight of the Lord, according to all that his father David had done.
>
> 4He removed the high places and broke down the sacred pillars and cut down the Asherah. He also broke in pieces the bronze serpent that Moses had made, for until those days the sons of

Israel burned incense to it; and it was called Ne-hushtan.

2 Kings 18:3-4

The bronze serpent, once the instrument of the miraculous power of God, was now worshipped as an idol.

Once a missionary came back to America from a country that was starving. What they needed more than anything else was a well and a pump to get the water out of the ground. They were Christians, and they needed help. So the missionary raised thousands of dollars to dig that well and put a pump on it. It was wonderful. The water flowed, and the crops began to grow, and they were saved from famine and starvation.

Soon after the well and irrigation system were installed, the missionary went home on furlough. When he returned, he was shocked to find the people had made a shrine and were worshipping the pump.

Being a Purpose-driven Person

I surprise people when I say that I am not a goal-driven person. They wonder how we could have ever built such a church, started so many outreach ministries and accomplished so much.

I certainly know where I'm going, but I don't dwell on the end goal. Purpose drives my life. It is my purpose to win lost people to Jesus Christ. That's what motivates me every day.

The vision and goal are clear, but they're put away and are seldom reviewed. You see, what you dwell on every day, what drives and motivates you, the thing that becomes the central focus of your life, can easily become something that you worship. And when we start to worship our dreams, visions and goals, it's very hard to lay them on the altar.

For preachers the goal might be a large church. For

others the vision might be for success in business or athletics or living in a more affluent neighborhood. We also have plans and goals for our children.

None of these things is wrong. But if you are looking for a miracle in your house to enable you to fulfill your dreams, you might not find it until you are willing to put those dreams on the altar.

Your vision cannot become your idol. As a young man I dreamed of pastoring a great church. Through the years I didn't ask every day when it was going to come to pass. I didn't think every day, I'm working toward the vision. It was just there in my subconscious. I didn't fret; I was enjoying the trip. I was happy abiding in the Lord. If it was His vision, He would bring it to pass.

One day I looked up at our church sanctuary and realized something. It was what I had envisioned when I was a young man. I marveled to myself: Well, it did come to pass after all.

I am amazed that I am living in the vision I had years ago. But it has not been an idol, and I have not been obsessed with it. The trip has been more enjoyable than the destination.

Ungrasping Assurance

One of the greatest feelings is to know that what you are doing is God's idea and not your own. If you're doing God's thing, then you have even more assurance that He is going to be with you to help you bring it to pass.

One of the questions most asked of pastors is this: How do you know if what you are wanting to do is just your desire or God's plan?

It's hard to have assurance that it's from God until you put those plans and dreams on the altar. But when the sense of God's guiding is still there after you've laid those things before Him repeatedly with a willing heart to let them go, then you begin to have that assurance.

You can say, This is not my idea. I laid it on the altar many times. This is God's plan, and I feel it's my duty to obey.

At first you hold on to the vision. Eventually, the vision begins to hold on to you. You couldn't let it go if you wanted to. They say if you keep a vision for five years, it will come to pass. But most people cannot keep a vision for five years. They get discouraged and give up.

I could have grasped for my dream of a large church and missed the miracle of the tiny church in Davenport. I could have refused to leave Davenport and missed the miracle of Phoenix. I could have lost my ability to minister because of my heart problem. Nevertheless, I laid all those plans and dreams on the altar and found that each time God had a miracle in store for me. The miracle was in the bush.

TWELVE

The Interval Between Promise and Miracle

GOD SPEAKS to people in many ways — sometimes through the Bible; other times through people, through dreams, through visions or through an inner intuition we know as the still, small voice.

However it comes, when a person receives a promise from God, there is usually an interval of time between the promise and the manifestation or fulfillment of that promise. Whether it is a day or years or a lifetime, waiting for God to come through with your miracle can be an agonizing struggle. God is not forgetful, and He's not too busy to attend to the things concerning you. He has a definite purpose for all that He does, even for the delays. So it is important that we know how to respond to God in the interval between promise and miracle. Here are a few things to remember:

1. There Is an Appointed Time for Everything

God's clock doesn't seem to operate like mine. I always want to see the answer immediately. Sometimes that happens, but it's not the norm. I've come to learn that there is a difference between what I mean when I say *now* and what God means when He says *now*. For God, *now* is the point He speaks or wills something to be done. It makes no difference whether it has happened in our realm of reality or not. If He wills it, it is so. It is as good as done. For us, *now* is not until we see the physical manifestation.

How God's foreknowledge and His predetermination factor into the outworking of His will in our lives is beyond our knowing. Some have said that, for us, it's like watching a grand parade through a knothole in the fence. We see all the bands and floats go by one by one. But for God it is as if He sits atop the highest point and looks over the fence to see the entire parade from beginning to end — all at once. For the eternal God, the whole parade of history is *now*.

It's difficult for me, one who lives totally within this world of time and sequence of events, to understand God and His timing. Yet I know there is an appointed time for all things.

Paul in his sermon to the philosophers at Mars Hill said that it was God who "determined their [the nations'] appointed times, and the boundaries of their habitation" (Acts 17:26). He also said: "He has *fixed a day* in which He will judge the world in righteousness through a Man whom He has appointed" (Acts 17:31, italics added).

Part of the reward for Christ's suffering was that He

would be made Lord of heaven and earth and that at His judgment seat every knee would bow. That is without a doubt a promise from the Father that, from God's perspective, is already done. But God has *fixed a day* on which the actual event will take place and the fulfillment of the promise to the Son shall be manifest.

God also has a time appointed for the fulfillment of the promise He has made to you. If God has promised it, in a very real sense it is already done.

GOD HAD AN APPOINTED time for the fullness of Abraham's promise. When Abram was seventy-five years old, God gave him a promise — that from him would come a great nation (Gen. 12:1-3).

But time went by, and there was no child.

The promise was repeated again in more specific terms:

> THEN behold, the word of the Lord came to him, saying, "This man [Abram's servant, Eliezer] will not be your heir; but one who shall come forth from your own body, he shall be your heir."
>
> Genesis 15:4

Perhaps at that time Abram was tired of believing for the child and was willing to settle for something else and rationalize that it was God's answer. The Lord said, "No, it's going to be a child of your own."

More time passed — twenty-four years to be exact — and still no child. "I am the God Almighty," the Lord said the next time He spoke to him.

Abram may have thought, Yeah, I'm Abram, and I'm ninety-nine years old. I thought I was going to be a father.

At this meeting God changed Abram's name to Abraham, which means "the father of a multitude" (Gen. 17:5). It was a strange name for a man almost one hundred years old with no children.

The people who knew Abram, who now called himself

Abraham, must have been snickering in their tents, "The old man now calls himself the father of a great multitude." It would seem that the struggle of faith in the interval period had finally gotten to old Abe.

The Lord appeared to Abraham and repeated the promise for the third time. He said:

> IS anything too difficult for the Lord? At the appointed time I will return to you, at this time next year, and Sarah shall have a son.
>
> Genesis 18:14

The miracle had been for an appointed time all along. But as far as God was concerned, it was already done, because He had already willed it, spoken it and even foreseen it. For God, Abraham had always been the father of a multitude.

God has His timetable, and His appointed times are probably not affected very much by our begging and pleading. Abraham, in his frustration over God's timing, tried to make the promise happen by conceiving a son with his maidservant Hagar. You would think that God would have speeded things up to keep Abraham from making such a mistake. No, God had His time, and His time had a purpose.

Solomon said it most beautifully:

> THERE is an appointed time for everything. And there is a time for every event under heaven —
>
> 2A time to give birth, and a time to die;
> A time to plant, and a time to uproot
> what is planted....
>
> 9What profit is there to the worker from that in which he toils?
> 10I have seen the task which God has given the sons of men with which to occupy themselves.

¹¹He has made everything appropriate in its
time. He has also set eternity in their heart.
Ecclesiastes 3:1-2,9-11

2. God Is Preparing *You*
for the Miracle

Most of us would like to run to heaven's bank to cash in
on a promise before the day is done. Why does God make
it so difficult? Why doesn't He make things happen
sooner? Why must we struggle through this interval between promise and fulfillment?

There's a good answer to that, but you may not like it.

It is to perfect our faith and to give it endurance (see
James 1:2-4; 1 Peter 1:6-7). If we all said what we thought,
many of us would reply, "I don't care about having my faith
perfected. I just need a miracle, and I need it right now!"

Most of the time when we struggle with God it is because
we don't see things from His perspective. The quality and
enduring nature of our faith is of relatively little value to us,
compared to the supreme importance God places on it. It is
to Him more valuable than our good works, our comfort or
even our lives. It was Abraham's faith that was counted as
righteousness (Gen. 15:6). It is our faith that brings us salvation and all the promises of our inheritance.

We are always in a hurry to get on with God's plan for
our lives, but God's first order of business is dealing with
our faith. It is through these intervals, the periods between the promise and the miracle, that this "most holy
faith" is perfected (Jude 20).

Abraham was not the only person in the Bible to have
his faith operated upon. Jacob waited many years for the
promised birthright. His efforts to speed up the process
by stealing it from his brother accomplished nothing to
speed up the process. He should have learned that from
his grandfather's example.

Joseph had to wait and endure much as an Egyptian

slave before his dreams came to pass.

There were many years and a lot of troubles between the time David was anointed as king by Samuel and the day he actually came to sit on the throne.

Each of these biblical figures received a promise but went through a lot in the interval. They were all changed in the process and prepared to receive the promise. That may not be very important to you, but it's the highest order of business to God. In fact, it's the most important thing for you, too. It's just that often you don't realize it.

3. You Need to Prepare Yourself for the Miracle

King Sennacherib of Assyria invaded Judah during the fourteenth year of the reign of Hezekiah, king of Judah. Sennacherib's messenger, taunting Hezekiah, said:

> NOW therefore, come make a bargain with my master the king of Assyria, and I will give you two thousand horses, if you are able on your part to set riders on them.
>
> Isaiah 36:8

That Scripture passage has for years stuck in my mind because it reminds me of one of the first principles I learned concerning the kingdom of God. That principle is: If you just learn to ride, God will give you a horse. In other words, if you will prepare yourself for God's promise, He will bring it to pass.

WHEN I WAS ONLY four years old, God gloriously came into my heart and saved me. By the time I was ten years old, I knew that I was called to be a preacher. I began to prepare my life for that great event.

At the age of thirteen I would go out in the woods and preach from the tree stumps. I remember the time when

I got my buddies together in one of the old buses at my dad's church and preached a sermon complete with an altar call. Some of my friends were saved that way.

I remember going into the church auditorium, locking the doors, turning on the public address system and preaching to the empty pews. One day I forgot to lock the back door. A man who lived on the street saw the lights and walked in. He saw that no one was there listening to the preacher; but since he had nothing else to do, he sat down and listened to the message. When I gave the altar call, he raised his hand to be saved. So I said, "I want all of you who raised your hands to come forward, from the left to the right, from the front to the rear of this building." The man stood and came forward to receive Christ along with my multitude of imaginary converts.

I would often go down to the mission and preach to the alcoholics and transients. That's one of the reasons why I love those people so much today. I was just a kid, not a minister or a preacher. I was learning how to ride, even though I didn't have a horse.

When I was sixteen years of age, I held my first revival in Seminole, Texas. Some might say that is when my ministry began. Actually, it began at ten years old when I received the promise. But during the interval between the promise and the manifestation, I was learning how to ride. Pretty soon God gave me a horse.

You may feel God has spoken to you about getting married. Even if you don't know who the lucky person is, prepare yourself. Read books; go to seminars; prepare your finances. Whatever the promise may be, do something to put your faith into action. Prepare yourself by learning how to ride.

4. Be Careful How You Claim the Promises

It can be terribly disappointing to spend years believing for a promise only to find that it was not God's promise to you, but something you just claimed for yourself. We must be careful how we claim promises.

The Scriptures record what God had to say to certain people in the context of their situations. Those words often contain promises that a Christian can claim and apply to his or her situation. However, it's helpful to get advice from pastors and other mature Christians concerning which verses or promises you should accept as a promise from God for yourself. In the end, however, you alone are going to have to discern what God is saying to you.

One of the ways the callings and promises of God are confirmed is in the process of learning to ride without the horse. If you think God has spoken to you and given you a promise, do something as an act of faith. If you believe He's told you that you will go to the mission field, in the interval while you are waiting for the open door, study foreign culture and language, reach out to the internationals in your city, and pray for the nations. If you go to the mission field, you know you'll have to clean out that sock drawer. So go ahead and clean it out.

It *would* be foolish to do something like quitting your job presumptuously. Many people have made mistakes because they got ahead of God's appointed time. But do what you can until God opens the door to take a further step.

Many people are waiting for a promise but not preparing for it to come to pass. The rudder on a ship does no good unless the ship is moving. It is in the process of doing what you can, stepping out in faith and learning to ride that God's calling and promises are either confirmed or redirected in your heart.

The interval between the promise and the manifestation can be a difficult struggle. But remember that God has His appointed time, and if He has said it, it will surely come to pass. In this interval of time let God do His perfect work in your faith. As for you, get busy learning to ride.

THIRTEEN

❖

Whatever He Says
to You, Do It

IT SEEMS that almost everyone looks for a method —
for healing, church growth, success in business, re-
pairing broken relationships and so on.

Many will travel to the ends of the earth to attend a
conference that will show them step-by-step how to be
successful in one area or another.

"I need a miracle, and I want to be able to put my finger
on exactly how to make it happen for me."

I suppose it would be much easier to reduce everything

to formulas, but that's not how it works with God. That's not how it works in life either. Methods and formulas enable us to calculate long-term strategies and manage risk. But they also offer the hope of results without the trouble of a relationship with God.

Good ideas, methods and even the examples of others' successes by themselves are like a fine-tuned engine without any gasoline. It is God who fuels our efforts and turns our dreams into reality. This is the most important part of the making of miracles — it is God who is the miracle maker.

There are two more stories of miracles in the house that I want to talk about. The first took place at a wedding.

AND on the third day there was a wedding in Cana of Galilee, and the mother of Jesus was there;

²and Jesus also was invited, and His disciples, to the wedding.

³And when the wine gave out, the mother of Jesus said to Him, "They have no wine."

⁴And Jesus said to her, "Woman, what do I have to do with you? My hour has not yet come."

⁵His mother said to the servants, "Whatever He says to you, do it."

⁶Now there were six stone waterpots set there for the Jewish custom of purification, containing twenty or thirty gallons each.

⁷Jesus said to them, "Fill the waterpots with water." And they filled them up to the brim.

⁸And He said to them, "Draw some out now, and take it to the headwaiter." And they took it to him.

⁹And when the headwaiter tasted the water which had become wine, and did not know where it came from (but the servants who had drawn

the water knew), the headwaiter called the bridegroom,

¹⁰and said to him, "Every man serves the good wine first, and when men have drunk freely, then that which is poorer; you have kept the good wine until now."

John 2:1-10

As the years went by, no matter how many times they refilled those waterpots, the water would never again be turned to wine. No matter how many times the widow would try to reproduce the circumstance that led up to her miracle, she just couldn't get the oil to multiply in her little bottle.

It wasn't the type of waterpots they refilled or the arrangement of the borrowed vessels or time of day she poured the oil. In each case what caused the miracle to occur is that the people did what the Lord said. If there is any formula here at all, it is that obedience to the Lord is the essential ingredient for the making of miracles.

The angel Gabriel, after telling Mary she would conceive a child by the Holy Spirit, said to her, "For nothing will be impossible with God" (Luke 1:37). Literally, the verse reads, "No word shall be impossible with God." The Greek word *rhema* which is used in this verse refers to the spoken word. Whatever God speaks to you is possible.

There's always a miracle in the house somewhere, but it's not always in the same place, and it often does not occur in the same way twice. We must be careful how we presume upon God's directions.

On one occasion, Moses was commanded to take the staff in his hand and strike the rock. He did so, and water came out (Ex. 17:6). Later he was told to speak to the rock, but he just went ahead and struck it as he had done before. When Moses used his staff in disobedience, it cost him his trip to the promised land (Num. 20:7-13).

We can't operate on someone else's vision or methods. We have to get a firsthand revelation from God ourselves. At our conference each year over five thousand pastors and church leaders listen for days to us talk about our 180 different ministries, special event days and hundreds of other ideas that have worked for us in Phoenix. But in the final session I tell them to go and get God's plan for themselves. They have to have a firsthand revelation of what God wants them to do.

On the last night we all go out to the mountain on the backside of our property, where we make a large cross out of hundreds of candles. The mountainside is filled with people singing and crying out to God for their own direction. You can hear it all night for miles.

To do it just the way I've done it, I tell them, might be like young David putting on Saul's armor. It just didn't fit. God was wanting to do something miraculous through David but in a totally different way.

Victory is not in methods but in miracles. Mary gave the best advice of all: Whatever He says to you, do it!

THERE IS ONE FINAL story in the Bible about miracles we need to consider. This time the miracle was in the boat.

The multitude pressed hard around Jesus to hear His every word. Seeing two boats at the edge of the lake of Gennesaret, He asked the fishermen who were washing their nets to put out a little way from the land so that He could preach from the boat. The boat belonged to Simon, who was also called Peter.

> AND when He had finished speaking, He said to Simon, "Put out into the deep water and let down your nets for a catch."
>
> [5]And Simon answered and said, "Master, we worked hard all night and caught nothing, but at

Your bidding I will let down the nets."

⁶And when they had done this, they enclosed a great quantity of fish; and their nets began to break.

Luke 5:4-6

In the making of every miracle are faith, obedience and the willingness to take a risk. These represent for you the three hurdles that you must overcome: doubt, fear and thinking you know it all.

It would have been much easier to ignore Jesus' suggestion, rather than to load the nets up again into the boat. Fishing all night tends to wear you out. Simon and his coworkers had no reason to believe they would catch anything — except that Jesus said to do it.

What did Jesus know about fishing anyway? They were the experts. Sometimes we become prisoners of our knowledge and expertise. I have heard so many people, church growth authorities included, tell me at every juncture that what I was attempting to do wouldn't work. The miracle happened anyway — but not because I was so smart. I had no reason to believe it would work either. I had nothing on which to base my faith except that I felt God said to do it.

Some people are addicted to impossibility thinking. For them nothing is going to work — ever! All they can see are the problems, the obstacles and every possible thing that could go wrong. Oftentimes such a negative, cynical perspective is rooted in a failure or a series of past failures.

Cynics are disillusioned idealists. Somewhere along the line something didn't work out for them. They became disillusioned and have been rehearsing their disappointment ever since. They have become shipwrecked with regard to their faith. Every promise of God and every hope and expectation for miracles are qualified or even discounted by the memory of their past disappointments.

It is as if they had fished all night and caught nothing. So why should they try anymore?

PAUL, AT THE END of his ministry, said to his friends in Philippi:

> BRETHREN, I do not regard myself as having laid hold of it yet; but one thing I do: forgetting what lies behind and reaching forward to what lies ahead,
> ¹⁴I press on toward the goal for the prize of the upward call of God in Christ Jesus.
>
> Philippians 3:13-14

Paul said that forgetting what lies behind was the *one thing* he did. We need to see how important forgetting really is.

If you ponder the past, your life will be shaped by it. What you hold in your memory, you will see in your experience. But if you are going to start walking in victory and newness of life, you have to forget how you have lived a life of limitation, failure and futility.

How do you know what it is you haven't forgotten? Tell me what you think about all the time, and I'll show you what you haven't forgotten. If it's constantly on your mind, it will constantly be in your experience.

Let me tell you something. Attitude is everything. The world is full of people with wounded faith, and if you happen to be one of them, today is the day to stop living in the past. You need to forget your failure and go on.

Remembering the past is a habit. Habits take time to form and discipline to break. One of the best ways you can change is to cultivate new thoughts. You can't think about two things at once. So get a new thought to crowd out the old.

Paul was reaching for the ultimate, so he had to forget what lay behind and press on. God has a great purpose for your life, so don't sit back nursing your memories. Be like Simon Peter who said, "We worked hard all night and caught nothing, *but at Your bidding* I will let down the nets" (Luke 5:5, italics added).

Launch Out Into Deep Water

Jesus said to Peter, "Put out into the deep water and let down your nets for a catch" (Luke 5:4). Though the depth of the water presented no danger at the time for the fishermen in the boat, remember that it was this same Simon Peter who later took a dangerous step out of the boat in the midst of a storm to walk on the water.

For us, deep water can be symbolic of taking a substantial risk. The greatest hindrance to walking by faith is trying to be fail-safe. Methods and formulas are for people who want to calculate their risk. But following God is totally unpredictable. Abraham left Ur of the Chaldees without a plan or a road map. He was just obeying the voice.

People are longing for God to work in their lives or perform miracles in their situations. The problem for many is that if He speaks, they won't do anything. If He challenges them, they will not take the risk.

When the challenge comes, they say, I just need one more sign and one more confirmation. Some have hundreds of words and confirmations. There's no sense talking about asking God for a miracle if you're not going to do anything when you hear from Him.

Every time I've found a miracle in the house, it's because I took the risk and obeyed the leading. Every time I've released people to take charge, it's a big risk. What if they fail? What if they are unfaithful? What if the water's too deep, and they're in over their heads? Well, we'll be in trouble. But I'll never know and they'll never know until they take the plunge. So many times as a pastor I just pray, lead the cheers and hold on for the ride. Every time we plan a big event, try a new idea or reach out to a new group of people, we take a risk. What if the miracles stop?

I believe in people, and I believe in miracles. As long as we have kept pouring, the fresh oil has kept multiplying. God will do that for you, too.

It's not just that God wants to give you a miracle; He wants to make you a miracle in someone else's life, too. That's where the greatest joy of all comes from. Remember: the more you're spilled, the more you are filled.

So make the decision to be a giver and a pourer. You may just discover that the miracle's in the house.

Forget what lies behind.

Step out into the deep.

Find some empty vessels and start pouring.

And whatever He says to you, do it.

QUESTIONS FOR DISCUSSION OR REFLECTION

CHAPTER 1

DOWN AND OUT
IN DAVENPORT

Focus: Identify the Need

Read Mark 4:30-32.
There's a Miracle in Your House! introduces principles to show believers how to trust God for a miracle that will solve a problem or meet a challenge.

We can apply these principles to the problems and challenges we have experienced, or will experience, thus turning them into opportunities for a miracle to take place. But we cannot do so without trusting God for the outcome.

1. For many believers, learning to trust God in difficult situations, rather than coming up with our own solutions, is not easy to do. Can you recall a time when you took your hands off a problem and trusted God to solve it? How was His solution better than any you could have chosen?

2. What is one of the greatest spiritual challenges you've ever faced? (Witnessing to a family member? Standing up for what you believe? Exercising spiritual gifts? etc.)

3. Have you ever felt that God was testing or challenging you to spiritual growth through a problem or crisis? If so, what was being tested?

4. Tommy Barnett states, "God's miracles are found behind some uninviting doors." What life situation led you through an "uninviting door" ultimately to experience one of your greatest spiritual victories?

5. Is there some area of your life where you're "down and out"? What is it? As you continue studying this book, imagine yourself placing that area in your hand, lifting it up to God and trusting Him to work a miracle in your life.

> *"In the midst of impossible*
> *situations I have just kept saying,*
> *'There's got to be a miracle in the house!'*
> *And God comes through — sometimes in*
> *ways I could never have imagined."*

CHAPTER 2

TELL ME — WHAT DO
YOU HAVE IN THE HOUSE?

Focus: Ten Principles for the Making of a Miracle

Read 2 Kings 4:1-7.

We can learn to see the sufficiency of God in each life situation. Using the story of the widow with a little jar of oil, this chapter has identified ten principles which can revolutionize the believer's life. They can become the ten ingredients for the making of a miracle.

> *Principle 1:* Know Where to Go When You Don't Know What to Do.
> *Principle 2:* Don't Seek an Earthly Messiah.
> *Principle 3:* Find Out What's in the House.
> *Principle 4:* Don't Be Blinded by Negativism, but Pass on to the Positive.
> *Principle 5:* Faith Is Not Faith Until You Do Something — Action Is Required.
> *Principle 6:* Don't Put Limitations on God's Ability to Provide.
> *Principle 7:* Shut the Door on Doubt.
> *Principle 8:* Pour Until There Is No More.
> *Principle 9:* Move Beyond the Miracle.
> *Principle 10:* Remember: There Will Always Be Enough.

1. Elisha asked the widow who needed a miracle, "What do you have in the house?" Take time to ask God what

154

you have in the house that might be the beginning of your miracle. It may be as simple as the widow's little jar of oil. Does the church you attend have a "little jar of oil" that could become a mighty miracle?

2. Some problems are so big that the only hope or option is trusting God for a miracle. Other problems seem more manageable — and can be worked out by human effort. Which is more difficult for you: trusting God with the big problems or trusting God with the little problems? Why?

3. Rehearsing our problems mentally keeps us focused on the problem rather than on the Problem-Solver. What is the difference between thinking about a problem and praying about a problem?

4. How does running to one person after another to discuss our problems hinder us from recognizing the solution?

5. When Elisha sent the widow to her neighbors he told her to get more jars, thus enabling the neighbors to become a part of her miracle. Rather than talking about her problem, they worked with her on a solution. Who has become a part of a miracle in your life? Who could be a part of a miracle you need right now?

> *"Like the needy widow we get so caught up*
> *in what we don't have that we do not see*
> *the possibilities in what we already have...*
> *She did not need a new vision of her need...*
> *What she needed was to recognize that God had*
> *already given her the beginnings for her miracle,*
> *even though what she had seemed so small."*

CHAPTER 3

BEING LED TO
YOUR NEXT MIRACLE

Focus: Learn to Recognize God's Miracle Game Plan

Read 1 Kings 17:1-16.

A wadded-up letter in a trash can was part of God's strategy for a miracle, but Tommy Barnett almost failed to recognize it. Ravens and a dried-up brook were included in God's game plan for Elijah. God's process of miracle making is accompanied by a never-ending series of unusual and unexpected things.

1. Elijah thought a brook was the solution to his problem, but it dried up just before he was led to his next miracle. Have you ever grieved over something that dried up or ended only to discover that God was preparing something new for you?

2. Instead of receiving "heavenly" food from the hands of angels, Elijah was fed by dirty birds. What surprising providers has God used to bring about a miracle in your life?

3. Tommy Barnett says, "One of the hardest lessons in life is to learn that God calls us to a place for a reason and for a season." Think of the following "surprise moments" in your life. Choose one of them and relate the reason and the season for it:

- A surprising place in which you've ended up?

- A surprising problem?

- A surprising provision?

- A surprising directive?

4. At times, our response to God in the moment just before a miracle comes can determine if that miracle occurs. For example, what if the widow had refused to prepare the little cake for Elijah? Do you think the miracle would have taken place? Can you recall a time when your response to God either hindered or allowed a miracle in your life?

5. A flashlight only shines a short distance in front. As you continue to walk, more of the path is lighted. That's what it's sometimes like to follow God's leading. You see one step at a time.

What would you say to encourage someone concerning God's step-by-step guidance? Do you have a personal story?

> *"God can and will provide from*
> *unusual sources by surprising means...*
> *The answer to a desperate need came*
> *from a 'miracle in the house.'*
> *Miracles are not magic — but multiplication.*
> *Obedience to His Word and faith*
> *in His promise put what we have into*
> *the Lord's hands so it can be multiplied."*

CHAPTER 4

WHAT'S THAT IN YOUR HAND?

Focus: The Seed for Your Miracle Is in Your Hand

Read Exodus 4:1-5.

Moses implored God to deliver the Israelites from slavery in Egypt. Yet when God replied, "Why don't *you* deliver them, Moses," he vacillated in his willingness to do as God suggested. Many times our lack of complete trust in God (and in our own abilities) keeps us from recognizing that the seed for the miracle we need is within our own grasp.

1. Read 2 Corinthians 12:9, a verse about power being perfected in weakness. How do we tap into God's power in our moments of weakness?

2. What character qualities do you possess into which you would most like to see God pour His power? Are these your strongest or weakest qualities? With God's power your weakest character trait can become your strongest gift.

3. Just as a diamond is created from the pressure and stress placed upon it, we often develop our strongest and most gifted character traits from the pressures and stresses life brings to us. Recall a very stressful period of your life. What character traits developed as a result of that experience?

4. Although God creates each of us with unique abilities and character qualities, people around us often attempt to force us into prescribed roles. This happened to Tommy Barnett's mother, Joy, who couldn't play the guitar or sing. Have you ever felt boxed in by people's expectations? If so, how did you feel? Did it hinder or help you to take steps to become the unique person God created you to be?

5. You need a miracle when: 1) troubles are forced upon you; 2) you accept the challenge to meet a need. Are you in either of these situations? Describe it.

*"When faced with desperate needs
and overwhelming challenges,
look to God and ask Him to help you
see if the seed of your miracle is already
in your hand. When you recognize it,
offer it to God in faith that the works of God
would be displayed through you."*

CHAPTER 5

FINDING THE MIRACLE WITHIN

Focus: Planting the Seed to a Miracle

Read Ephesians 4:7-8,11 and Romans 12:6-8.
The author states, "Inside every human being is a miracle waiting to be discovered and released." The Scripture passages above tell us God has given each of us different gifts according to His grace. But just as a diamond in a diamond mine is useless until it is discovered, so our unique gifts and abilities lie dormant until we release them into service.

1. Tommy Barnett made a distinction between a burden (something you don't want to do) and calling (something you want to do). Whether or not we release our gifts into service may depend on whether we consider them burdens or callings. What gifts do you feel burdened to use? ("I know I should teach a Sunday school class." "I guess I had better witness to that person." "I really ought to sing in the choir.")

   What gifts do you feel called to use? ("I would love to use my ability to teach." "I want that person to know what Jesus did for me." "I want to use my voice to praise God.")

   Notice how your outlook determines whether you have a burden or a calling.

2. At times, what motivates us to serve is not the fear of judgment if we don't use our gifts, but the desire to feel the grace of God working through us. Which gifts do you use because you fear God's judgment if you don't? Which gifts give you great pleasure to use because of God's grace? Why?

3. Tommy Barnett says, "Even when a person shows no outward signs of potential at all, I just believe it's there. Each person has a special grace and calling." Do you know someone who seems to have no potential? What will you do to show that you believe in them?

4. How does sin make it harder for us to know God's plan for our lives?

> *"I am convinced that every*
> *Christian has the innate desire*
> *to do something great for God,*
> *to lay down at the foot*
> *of the cross the biggest gift*
> *he or she possibly can...*
> *I believe in people."*

CHAPTER 6

HOW MANY LOAVES
DO YOU HAVE?

Focus: We Plant, But God Brings the Harvest

Read Mark 6:37-44.

We may open our hands to expose the seed of a miracle with great apprehension. But if we release it, God will miraculously bring a great harvest beyond our comprehension. Perhaps that is the greatest miracle — being willing to release the seed.

1. a. "Some look at the growing critical needs [in our world] and conclude that they are more than the church can handle."

    b. "The church has all the resources it needs to show the love of Christ to the world, and those resources are already sitting in the pews."

    Do you agree with the first or second statement. Why?

2. The people who attended that first Thanksgiving dinner at First Assembly made the congregation uncomfortable. The church people had to confront their willingness to accept whoever responded in spite of any perceived differences. Are there areas of ministry at your church which have created the same opportunity for you to grow spiritually — for example, ministry to the divorced, AIDS victims, the homeless and so on?

3. The author relates that each year the church members bring so much food to the Thanksgiving dinner that they are able to give leftovers to community soup kitchens. Thus their miracle is expanded to become the miracle for many others also. Have you ever watched God expand your miracle to others? How did this happen?

4. At a communion service, Tommy Barnett asked if everyone in the congregation had been served. He had prearranged to have several members of the congregation speak out about groups that the church could serve better, such as the handicapped and the homeless. Then, to his surprise, others in the congregation stood and mentioned other groups that needed to be served. Which groups would you have mentioned that day?

5. The seeds for miracles within our communities and churches are often already in place within the talents, skills and gifts of the people in the congregation. As a group, brainstorm for a list of resources your church has which have yet to be utilized as seeds for miracles.

"In the next ten years there is going to be
an abundance of needy people in our society —
and not just with financial needs.
There will be divorce; broken homes;
incurable diseases like AIDS; all kinds of abuse,
addictions and emotional problems;
a growing number of older people who need help;
and many with a general emptiness from
not knowing Jesus Christ as their Savior.
What a great time and a great
opportunity for the church.
That's our mission —
to show the love, grace and power
of Jesus to a hurting world."

CHAPTER 7

MIRACLES ON MY DOORSTEP

Focus: Miracles in Shoes — Focusing on People

Read Luke 14:15-24.

Tommy Barnett refers to needy people as "miracles in waiting." He contributed much of his success in ministry in Phoenix to a time when he visited India. He was impacted by the eyes of the poor of Calcutta, "boring silently into me, pleading for help...What I had witnessed would haunt me forever."

1. Have you experienced a time when you were gripped by the needs of others around you? Was it a life-changing moment? How were you changed?

2. If you had an unlimited amount of time at your disposal, to what group of people would you like to reach out? What would you do for them?

3. Although we may be touched by the needs of others, our empathy alone will never be a solution to their problem. William Booth, founder of the Salvation Army, had a son named Bramwell. Bramwell once told his father about the men who were sleeping under the bridges of London. His father replied simply, "Why don't you do something about it?"

Has God ever said to you, "Why don't you do something about it?" Tell about the experience.

4. It's a challenge to think of needy people as assets instead of burdens. Can you think of a person who was an "outcast" and became a "mighty man of valor"?

5. Tommy Barnett confronts the issue of class consciousness among believers. He states: "When we care for the poor and powerless God blesses us with the prominent and powerful." In the New Testament Paul stated, "I have become all things to all men, that I may by all means save some" (1 Cor. 9:22). Have you struggled with class consciousness? How have you overcome it?

> *"The greatest revival is always among*
> *empty vessels. Those who consider themselves*
> *to be filled don't thirst for more.*
> *In most churches Christians spend*
> *too much time filling themselves.*
> *We must be careful not to become addicted*
> *to the self-gratification of our senses*
> *when there are so many empty vessels*
> *waiting to be filled."*

CHAPTER 8

DON'T LET TROUBLES KEEP YOU FROM THE MAKING OF A MIRACLE

Focus: Encountering Adversity and Trouble

Read Isaiah 43:1-3.

There's a miracle to be found in every situation. But you have to be careful not to let your troubles cause you to miss it. Believers will no doubt encounter just as many troubles as they will miracles — indeed, more! When disaster strikes and the miracle seems out of reach, we must learn to trust God and wait patiently for Him to work.

1. Tommy Barnett describes how he reacted to a situation where he was unjustly attacked. First, he felt hurt; then he wanted to fight; finally, he sought God's will. How do you react when you're falsely accused?

2. The author says, "When you're trying to fight the battle with your own strength...you are tempted to manufacture your own miracles." Have you ever tried to fight your own battles or manufacture your own miracles? What happened?

3. What looks like a bad situation can be made much worse by our attempts to make a miracle happen. A good example is when Abraham tried to produce an heir through Hagar. He brought pain and suffering not only to himself but also to his family. He even

hindered Ishmael and all his descendants from readily experiencing the blessing of God.

Have you ever hindered someone else from receiving a miracle by trying to manufacture your own miracle — for example, unforgiveness toward another, manipulating for a position someone else deserved or taking credit for someone else's work? What effect did it have on your relationship with that person?

4. In this chapter, the community protested the church's plans to build a prayer chapel on a mountain. How should a church respond when there is public disapproval for something it does?

5. Sometimes we let past failures interfere with receiving our miracles today. Are you being held back by past failures? What are they? Ask God to transform your failure into a stepping stone for a miracle.

6. Tommy Barnett refused to let unforgiveness get a grip on him when the *Wall Street Journal* printed an unfair article. His letter of forgiveness to the reporter, Rob Johnson, allowed him to move forward.

    What act of forgiveness have you extended to another person, thus freeing you from bitterness and unforgiveness over an unfair circumstance or situation?

*"You will get offtrack if you think you know for sure
exactly what kind of miracle God wants to give you.
Remember that miracles come from surprising places
in unexpected ways. You have to trust that God is
working all things together for good according to
His great plan. Do everything you can to flow
with His plan rather than trying
to force Him to bless yours."*

CHAPTER 9

PASS ON TO THE POSITIVE

Focus: Taking Your Thoughts Captive

Read Philippians 4:6-9 and Isaiah 26:3.
There's nothing like a big problem to muddy up a miracle in the making or to reveal the many carnal emotions we must release to God before the miracle can take place. In his account of his experience, Tommy Barnett shares many insights to help us as we face similar situations.

1. Tommy Barnett writes, "There is one thing that meditating on...your predicament will do for you. It will create a monster inside you." Then he asks, "Are you feeding any pet monsters in your life?" Think back to a time when you became upset because of an injustice against you. What negative feelings did you have to release before you could sincerely want God's will to be done in the situation?

2. "The fear of losing your job can take on a more destructive aspect in your life than the actual consequences of being laid off." What other fears can you think of that are more destructive than the thing that is feared?

3. Negative feelings and emotions are a product of the natural man. Miracles are a product of the supernatural. The two will never be compatible. But we can

replace our negative emotions and feelings with the fruit of the Spirit, thus teaming up with the Holy Spirit in the making of a miracle.

List the negative emotions you have experienced. Using Galatians 5:22-23, determine which fruit of the Spirit can be substituted for each negative emotion you listed.

4. Think about a problem or difficulty you face. Try imagining ten different ways God could work things out for you.

5. In Jeremiah 25:9, the evil King Nebuchadnezzar, who was tormenting Israel, was called God's servant. That introduces an interesting concept: Trouble can become your servant. Have troubles become your master or your servant? How have you learned to make them your servant?

   "God can solve a problem in a thousand ways...
   Don't consider your problems until you
   have the faith to see them from
   God's perspective...Don't grow
   a thought monster inside that you
   will have to feed forever."

CHAPTER 10

THE MORE YOU'RE SPILLED, THE MORE YOU'RE FILLED

Focus: The Holy Spirit in Our Lives

Read 1 John 4:7-21.

One of the remarkable concepts the book highlights is that the more we pour ourselves out into the lives of others, the more we can anticipate being filled and re-filled by the Holy Spirit. This is contrary to our human way of thinking. We know that if we have a full glass of water but spill half of it, we only have half a glass of water left. Yet as Spirit-filled believers, we stay Spirit-filled by spilling out to others. The miracle continues as long as we are "Spirit-spilled."

1. The idea of "spilling for a filling" causes us to consider the pattern of being refilled with God's Spirit in our own lives. Often we feel that we must be on a spiritual moun-taintop, completely filled with the Spirit, before we count ourselves ready to spill out in service to others. Yet it is as we empty ourselves out in service to others that a refilling often occurs. Think back to a time when you gave freely of yourself to help someone else. Did the Holy Spirit refill you immediately after the experience? Relate how you were renewed by the Spirit.

2. Have there been times when you felt unprepared spiritually to minister to others? Describe your re-sponse to these feelings.

3. Tommy Barnett likens the kingdom of God to the moisture in our air. He says believers are like the droplets of water that become visible when the air reaches the dew point. What are some of the ways you have helped the invisible kingdom of God to be seen in your world?

4. The author says that there are two ways to live: as a giver or as a taker. As you think about the gifts and abilities that God has given to you, list areas where you would like to find ways to use your gifts and abilities to help others. Are there any areas where you have been withholding your gifts and abilities?

5. Share about a time when someone poured themselves into your life at a moment of need. How did their example inspire you to become a giver?

"For the apostles, being filled
with the Holy Spirit was not something
that happened only once. It was an ongoing
occurrence that always resulted in
a demonstration of love and service to others.
No one has any need to be filled
unless he or she intends to be poured.
And the more you are poured,
the more you are refilled."

CHAPTER 11

THE MIRACLE'S IN THE BUSH

Focus: Worship the Miracle-Worker — Not the Miracle

Read Numbers 21:4-9 and 2 Kings 18:1-4.

God provided a ram for Abraham to sacrifice instead of his son, Isaac, and Abraham worshipped God for His provision. But when God healed the Israelites through means of a bronze serpent, they began to worship the serpent. We must not forget that the source of our miracles is God. We must worship Him and give Him first place in our lives — not the miracles He brings.

1. Five hundred years after Moses made the bronze serpent, Hezekiah broke it into pieces because the Israelites had given it a name and were burning incense to it as to a god. Discuss how the bronze serpent represents worshipping the miracle instead of the Miracle-Worker.

2. It is fairly easy to recognize when things or possessions become more important to us than God is. However it is harder to recognize when our goals, visions and dreams have become the focus of our worship. Discuss how the following could become too important to a believer:

   • Becoming a successful businessman

   • Moving into a bigger house

- Sending your children to a great university

- Building a successful outreach to one segment of society's needy people

- Dreaming of one day pastoring a large church

3. Tommy Barnett states: "One of the greatest feelings is to know that what you are doing is God's idea and not your own. If you're doing God's thing, then you have even more assurance that He is going to be with you to help you bring it to pass." Name something God gave you the idea to do. How did you recognize that it was God's idea for you? How did He work to bring it to pass? What did you have to do to help make it happen?

4. We must learn to become purpose-driven persons, not goal-driven people. The purpose is more important than the goal. For example, your *goal* may be to bring fifty people in wheelchairs to church, and your *purpose* is for them to receive salvation. You may only bring five people to church, but in the course of your visitation you lead fifty people to salvation. You missed your goal, but you're still on purpose. Can you think of a time when your goals changed but your purpose remained the same?

> *"If God has truly given you a promise,*
> *a vision, a gift or a ministry,*
> *you don't have to grasp for it.*
> *It is in His hands to bring it to pass.*
> *If you hold it too tightly,*
> *the gift can eventually become more precious*
> *to you than God who gave it."*

CHAPTER 12

THE INTERVAL BETWEEN PROMISE AND MIRACLE

Focus: Waiting for the Miracle to Happen

Read James 1:2-4 and 1 Peter 1:6-7.
When a person receives a promise from God, there is usually an interval of time between the promise and the manifestation or fulfillment of that promise. We must learn to respond properly to God in the interval between promise and miracle.

1. Waiting is not something we do easily. Even Abram grew impatient in the period of time between the promise of a son and the time when Isaac was born. After twenty-four years God reaffirmed to him, "At the appointed time...Sarah shall have a son" (Gen. 18:14). God's "appointed times" are not known by His people. Discuss the following:

   • What promises have you received from God for which you are waiting to see the miracle take place?

   • Abraham tried to hurry his miracle by having a child with Hagar, but it created problems for all concerned. How have you tried to hurry a miracle only to create distress or trouble?

   • Describe a time when you have had to wait for a promise to be fulfilled in your life. What did you do while you waited? How much time elapsed between the promise and the fulfillment?

2. Read Deuteronomy 29:29. How can you apply this verse to the interval between God's promise and God's miracle. What are the secret things? What has God revealed that can help you as you wait for your miracle?

3. Tommy Barnett had a promise from God that he would be a preacher. He prepared himself for the promise by preaching to his friends, to empty church pews and at the city mission. How can you prepare yourself for the promise?

4. Tommy Barnett asks the following questions: "Why does God make it so difficult? Why doesn't He make things happen sooner?" How would you answer these questions? One of the answers the author gives is that God does it to perfect our faith and to make it enduring. How have you learned endurance through waiting?

5. How can the believer keep from becoming discouraged and disappointed during the waiting? What portion of God's Word has been important for you when you were waiting for the fulfillment of a promise?

> *"Many people are waiting for a promise but not preparing for it to come to pass...The interval between the promise and the manifestation can be a difficult struggle. But remember that God has His appointed time, and if He has said it, it will surely come to pass. In this interval of time let God do His perfect work in your faith."*

CHAPTER 13

WHATEVER HE SAYS TO YOU, DO IT

Focus: Understanding God's Methods

Read Luke 5:1-7.

There is a carefully defined scientific method for conducting a scientific experiment and reaching a conclusion. Methods and formulas enable us to calculate long-term strategies and manage risk. But God does not make a miracle happen by using a method or formula. Each miracle He creates is the result of the supernatural, personal response of a God of love and compassion.

1. Tommy Barnett gives several biblical illustrations of miracles. He also states, "In each case what caused the miracle to occur is that the people did what the Lord said." Why do you think obeying the Lord is so important in the making of a miracle?

2. The purposes and methods God uses in any particular incident may seem strange or useless. The disciples had been fishing all night and had caught nothing when Jesus told them to put their nets in the water again. What would you have said to Jesus? What would you have done?

3. How God performs a miracle for your brother or sister may not be the way He chooses to bring a miracle into

your life. We must have a firsthand revelation of God's plan for our own lives and circumstances. What revelation of God's plan for *your* life has not yet come to pass? What has God revealed that He wants you to do to bring His plan to pass in your life?

4. Tommy Barnett makes the following statement: "In the making of every miracle are faith, obedience and the willingness to take a risk. These represent for you the three hurdles that you must overcome: doubt, fear and thinking you know it all."

    Recall a miracle in your life and share how you overcame the hurdle of doubt, the hurdle of fear and the hurdle of thinking you knew it all.

5. Another thought-provoking statement is this: "Every promise of God and every hope and expectation for miracles are qualified or even discounted by the memory of their past disappointments." Has your memory of past disappointment limited God from doing a miracle in your future? How can you begin walking in victory unhindered by past failures?

> *"I suppose it would be much easier*
> *to reduce everything to formulas,*
> *but that's not how it works with God...*
> *If there is any formula...at all,*
> *it is that obedience to the Lord*
> *is the essential ingredient*
> *for the making of miracles."*

NOTES

Chapter 3

1. From the hymn "Trust and Obey," text by John H. Sammis, music by Daniel B. Towner.

Chapter 5

1. Tom Peters and Robert Waterman, *In Search of Excellence: Lessons From America's Best Run Companies* (New York: Warner Books, 1982), p. 228.

2. *The New Strong's Exhaustive Concordance of the Bible* (Nashville, Tenn.: Thomas Nelson, 1984), Greek Dictionary of the New Testament, #264.

Chapter 6

1. "My Eyes Are Dry" by Keith Green, copyright © 1979 BMG Songs, Inc./Birdwing Music/Cherry Lane Music Co./Ears to Hear Music. All rights for Birdwing, BMG and Cherry Lane administered by BMG. All rights reserved. Used by permission.

Chapter 7

1. From "The Shoes of Happiness" by Edwin Markham (1852-1940). Reprinted from the book *Giant Hours With Poet Preachers*, compiled by William L. Stidger (New York: Abingdon Press, 1918).

Chapter 8

1. Editorial cartoon, *The Arizona Republic* (Phoenix), 18 September 1988.
2. Editorial, *The Arizona Republic* (Phoenix), 16 September 1988.
3. Ibid., 18 October 1988.
4. Editorial cartoon, *The Arizona Republic* (Phoenix), 18 October 1988.
5. Dee J. Hall, "Church's chapel plan irks neighbors," *The Arizona Republic* (Phoenix), 16 October 1988, section B.
6. Dee J. Hall, "Church's Tower Plan Is Derailed," *The Arizona Republic* (Phoenix), 19 October 1988, section A.
7. Ibid.

Chapter 10

1. John Rea, *The Holy Spirit in the Bible* (Lake Mary, Fla.: Creation House, 1990), pp. 293-294.
2. From the hymn "He Giveth More Grace," text by Annie Johnson Flint, music by Hubert Mitchell, copyright © 1941, renewed 1969 by Lillenas Publishing Co., Kansas City, MO 64141. All rights reserved. Used by permission.

You can experience more of *God's grace & love!*

*I*f you would like free information on how you can know God more deeply and experience His grace, love and power more fully in your life simply write or e-mail us. We'll be delighted to send you information that will be a blessing to you.

To check out other titles from **Creation House** that will impact your life, be sure to visit your local Christian bookstore, or call this toll-free number to learn the location of the Christian retailer nearest you: **1-800-991-7747**

For free information from Creation House:

CREATION HOUSE
600 Rinehart Rd.
Lake Mary, FL 32746
www.creationhouse.com